HE LOVES YOU, NOT

A Commonsense Guide to What NOT to do in Relationships

~

J.B. TREMONT

JB TREMONT, LLC
Delaware

Published by JB Tremont, LLC
P.O. Box 301, Glenside, Pennsylvania, 19038, U.S.A.

Copyright © by J.B. Tremont, 2011

Foreword by Richard A. Martin, M.A.
Senior Pastor, Life Community Church, 2011
All Rights Reserved

Library of Congress Control Number: 2010917317

JB Tremont, LLC ISBN 13 9780615473222
ISBN 10 0615473229

Printed in the United States of America

Cover design by Kevin Carr, New Media Dezines
Cover Photos by G.K. Clark, All Rights Reserved

Scriptures noted as KJV are taken from the King James Version. Copyright © 1994, Thomas Nelson, Inc., Publishers.
Scripture quotations marked NKJV™ are taken from the New King James Version®. Copyright © 1982 by Thomas Nelson, Inc. Used by permission. All rights reserved.
Scripture quotations marked NIV are taken from the Holy Bible, New International Version®, NIV®. Copyright © 1973, 1978, 1984 by Biblica, Inc.™ Used by permission of Zondervan. All rights reserved worldwide. www.zondervan.com

This book is sold subject to the condition that it shall not, by way of trade or otherwise, be lent, re-sold, hired out, or otherwise circulated without the publisher's prior consent in any form of binding or cover other than that in which it is published and without a similar condition including this condition being imposed on the subsequent purchaser.

www.jbtremont.blogspot.com
www.jbtremont.com

To my children
and my children's children.

To all young people (and those young at heart) who
feel as if they just do not have a clue.

FOREWORD

From our humble beginnings in the Bronx, New York and the mixing of our family life, to our faith in God now at the very center of our lives, I believe that JB and I continue to share in our life experiences, the move of God, to make things plain for our contemporaries. Through incredible life experience, we have traveled to a point of great blessings, both natural and spiritual. I know that JB would agree that through our respective platforms, we are afforded great opportunity to reach out to teach and inspire others to challenge and overcome their limits and achieve their highest possible purposes in life.

My cousin, no, more like my sister, has developed into a captain in the Lord's army setting straight these roads in a relationship that twist and turn people all in wrong directions. While I wish I could have been there for her through many bad situations as a brother should for his sister, it was almost necessary, my absence; to allow for this process to come to fruition, that we all might come to a better understanding of Godly relationships through her life experience.

With this book, JB Tremont systematically and with surgeon precision, picks apart at the indoctrinated lies and ploys of the enemy to bring light and life to the reader. It is an undeniable truth that one

Foreword

year from now, a person's life can be better or it can be worse, but it will never be the same. JB's book allows for your year in a relationship to be better if you will allow for the truths in these pages to speak life into you.

From the title of this book and within its pages, JB lays out the in-depth, but practical ground rules for engaging in relationships, rising above your fleshly desire and building upon your blessing of a healthy relationship. JB and her heart shared with us all; this serves as a model and guide for what we all need in life: good, sound wisdom.

Richard A. Martin M.A. Theology

PREFACE

Have you ever plucked a flower to determine whether "he loves you?" How often in your attempts to find love have you run out of petals hoping for one more? Oftentimes in life, there are no more petals and you are left with the pain associated with "he loves you, not."

    I never felt properly equipped with the necessary tools or adequate information to be successful in my relationships. From time to time, I glanced at dating articles in magazines, newspaper columns, and letters asking for advice on love, marriage, and dating. However, many times I attempted to find love, only to find that I was left with no more petals, and the heartache associated with an unsuccessful relationship. One that was resulting from showing up in a relationship unaware, ungrounded and unwhole. Consequently, I was in a number of sexual relationships, and a marriage that ended in divorce, so I am probably not the best candidate to offer my experience on relationships. But then again, given my history, maybe I am...

Preface

    I have contemplated what it takes to be in a successful relationship. I have had numerous discussions with men and women; college friends, co-workers, colleagues, married, single, teenagers to senior adults, and observed the rise and fall of countless relationships, due to the behavior of its participants. Yet, it was not until I experienced the love of Christ in my own life that I was able to heal from past hurts. I realized not knowing what <u>not</u> to do, or how <u>not</u> to act, is just as damaging to your relationship as knowing what to do, then acting inappropriately.

    So here are some tips that I have put together from the things that I did not know, but have learned along the way, and some that I wish I were taught. As you read, you might think to yourself, "this sounds like common sense." However, common sense is only common IF YOU KNOW IT and wisdom dictates that you apply it to your life. My hope is that you apply wisdom and common sense to your life.

Table of Contents

FOREWORD v

PREFACE vii

CHAPTER 1: A DATE IS JUST A DATE 1
    WHAT A DATE IS 2
    WHAT A DATE IS NOT 4
    HOW DO YOU DATE? 7

CHAPTER 2: SEX ON THE FIRST DATE 13

CHAPTER 3: LONG-TERM COMMITMENT 23

CHAPTER 4: TRUST YOUR GUT 45

CHAPTER 5: HEAR THOSE AROUND YOU 67

CHAPTER 6: SEX BEFORE MARRIAGE 77
    UNMARRIED SEX 78
    MARRIED SEX 81

CHAPTER 7: IF IT IS NOT WORKING, KNOW WHEN TO CALL IT QUITS 87
    WHY DO YOU HOLD ON? 88

CHAPTER 8: DO NOT FORCE IT, GET OFF THE RIDE 99
    RELATIONSHIP FLOW CHART 105

CHAPTER 9: OVERCOMING A BROKEN HEART 115

CHAPTER 10: LEARN TO LOVE YOUR SELF 125

CHAPTER 11: LUST DOES NOT (≠) EQUAL LOVE 139
    WHAT LUST IS 139
    WHAT LOVE IS 142

CHAPTER 12: WHAT MEN SAY 147

CONCLUSION 157

ACKNOWLEDGEMENTS 161

NOTES 163

INDEX OF A TO Z TOPICS 165

He Loves You, Not

Chapter 1: A Date is Just a Date

> *A date is a social or romantic appointment or engagement. It is two people who are usually attracted to one another, going out and getting to know each other [in that moment.]*[1]

I really did not know what a date was. In my house, we never discussed dating. Don't get me wrong, we talked about sex, birth control, and pregnancy, but never dating. Additionally, my father had a rule that I could not have a boyfriend until I was eighteen. (Oh, did I mention that my father was 6 feet, 5 inches tall, 260 lbs, and intimidated everyone who took me out on a date? Needless to say, they respected his "no boyfriend until 18," and that "I–will–kill–you–if–you–have–sex–with–my–daughter" rule?) Therefore, the implication was that I could date, but since dating was never a topic of discussion, I really did not understand what it meant to go on a date.

I had a preconceived idea that the definition of a date was going out with someone, to dinner or a movie. There was, of course, the anxiety associated with first, bad, or lasting impressions, <u>and that oh so important question pondered throughout the entire date: "will we kiss at the end??"</u> Nonetheless, the notion of a date was mainly gleaned from watching movies or television during my youth.

A "date" had a dual definition for me, not only did I think it was "going out" there was the sexual aspect included. My peers, other teens and young adults, also equated dating with having sex. I was confused, too. Although, I was interested in going out with a boy, that did not necessarily mean I was interested in having sex with him. Many people I have "dated" more times than not, defined dating as ultimately having sexual encounters. <u>But a date really is just a date.</u>

What a date is:

A date is a chance to go out with a person socially. Dating is sharing time with another person. There are various terms used to describe dating. When you consider just "talking," there is no commitment. At this stage, you are just talking to someone, usually by phone. You might see one another occasionally. When you begin "seeing" someone that means you are dating consistently, and contemplating a relationship. Now, "boo lovin" is quality time spent cuddled up with someone you nickname your "boo". A "boo" could be a friend, or someone you are dating.

No matter what term you use, dating should be a <u>casual</u> event. It should occur with regularity, and never burdensome. In the process, you get to know the man's character, his quirks, and flaws; the good, the bad, and the ugly. It really does take dating to get to know someone.

- <u>Dating gives you the opportunity to see what you have in common</u>. Dating is a data gathering process. Do you share the same tastes? What are his likes and dislikes? Do you have similar values? Do you share religious beliefs?

- <u>Dating gives you freedom</u>. When you date casually, you are not obligated to anyone, and there is no commitment, unless agreed upon. You are not obligated to have sex with him! You are not obligated to get to know him. If it does not work out, you can just walk away.

- <u>Dating allows you to weigh your options</u>. Dating on a regular basis gives you choices. If you are not interested in a man, you have the option to date someone else. By dating regularly, you can also avoid settling. Use this time productively to learn about yourself; what you like, what you expect, and what behavior you will or will not tolerate. Dating regularly will allow you to weed out men who do not meet your expectations without compromising your own.

Ideally, you want to become friends with the person with whom you plan to spend your time. And truth be told, you really do not "know" a person until you marry them…but that is for another book, another time.

What a date is not:

- <u>A date is not a long-term commitment</u>. It is a temporary entity. It is a preset engagement for an appointed time, which lasts for a certain, but limited duration. In fact, there is no commitment. You meet in order to go out, and even <u>that</u> is not set in stone. Consider how many times someone is "stood-up."

- <u>A date is not courtship</u>. If a man wants to marry you, he will court you. Courtship means he is pursuing you because he knows he wants a wife. He is pursuing you exclusively; he is pursuing you for marriage. If a man is not courting you, he is just dating you.

- <u>A date is not necessarily candidacy for marriage.</u> Given the temporary nature of a date, rarely does a single date determine your probability of marriage. As a woman, you can easily become preoccupied by that daydream, where only after <u>one</u> <u>date</u> you see yourself married, with children. After <u>one</u> <u>date,</u> you have planned your entire future with this man. You envision your house, your car, and your life with him while "Someday My Prince Will Come[2]" plays on your mental jukebox.

GET REAL! You do not know him. Come back to reality and see him for who he is. Do not allow your "dream" image of your date blind you to discovering who he really is.

Moreover, even if you are interested in finding a candidate for marriage, because you go on a date with someone does not mean that <u>he</u> is that candidate. GIVE YOURSELF SOME CREDIT. You are not that superficial or desperate. You do not want to marry <u>every</u> <u>man</u> you date, (nor are you interested in having his baby or "trapping" him – that is, getting him to be with you by purposely getting pregnant). Even if you are desperate, you do have standards.

- <u>A date does not automatically mean sex</u>. A date is not equivalent to sex. Going on a date with a man is not a definite indicator that you <u>want</u> to have sex. A man should not assume that because he bought you dinner, paid for a movie, or dancing, that you would automatically sleep with him. He should not <u>expect</u> sex from you. You do not owe him anything, and you are not obligated to "pay" him back.

Furthermore, sex adds another dynamic to the relationship. Sex creates vulnerability. You develop attachments. You may confuse lust for love. You may invest your emotions, which makes it easier for you to get hurt. It also becomes more difficult for you to move on when he shows lack of interest, or gives you the brush-off. Sex makes matters much more complicated.

How do you date?

There are various types of dates. You can go solo, on a blind date, or group dating.

- <u>Solo dating</u> occurs when you meet a man and agree to go on a date at an appointed time. There is usually some sort of communication prior to your engagement, via telephone, cell phone, or email. These conversations help you ascertain whether you will keep your date and if you are still interested in going out. Does he make you feel secure enough to be alone with him?

If the answer to any of these questions is no, then do not date him. Let him know that your date is a no-go.

- <u>A Blind date</u> is when your first date is the first time you meet. It is fair to say that if friends or family set you up on a blind date, they know you well enough to believe you and he might be compatible.

    Internet dating is also a form of a blind date. Whether you meet a person, in a chat room or a site designed for dating, there is something about your exchange that makes him appealing and compels you to want to meet.

    Occasionally, you are introduced by phone, prior to your date. This gives you the opportunity to develop a level of comfort before meeting. You can ask for a photo via email or cell phone or it may behoove you to Google him, and search him out on Facebook to see what information you can find on the social networking sites.

    Remember, no matter how your date is "set-up," this man is a stranger to you and there can exist an element of surprise. Be aware that blind dates are mostly cold sells, that is, you both are trying to convince a person you do not know to buy in to who you are. Good Luck!!!

- <u>Group dating</u> or double dating works best in a setting where there can be playful interaction, i.e. bowling, or a game party. You go out with another couple, or a group of friends and everyone can participate.

    Group dating takes some of the pressure off you individually. Since you and your date are usually familiar with another person in the group, you ultimately let down your guard. There is usually a lot of laughter, which affords you the opportunity to see a side of his personality that you may not have seen had you dated solo.

Let it be just a date. Now that you understand what dating is and is not, you are aware that there are tangible benefits to dating. So, I encourage you to date. Date often and date casually as the Lord leads you. There may be times when you are being worked on and molded to learn about yourself, so you will not repeat past mishaps. Try to go out to different venues and let him pay, you can pay, or split the cost. See if you <u>can</u> be friends with this person. If you cannot, cut your losses and move on. <u>This does not mean have sex</u>. Say goodbye and go home.

Do not give someone you just met every piece of personal information. He does not need to know your exact address, the name of the school you attend, the company you work for, or your work address. You can be evasive and speak in general terms when talking about where you live, what you do for a living, and where you work. For instance, "I live on the west side," "I'm in school," or "I work as an administrator for an insurance company." You do not want to disclose any information that would lead someone to track you down if that person turns out to be crazy, or a stalker. Give your cell phone number, instead of your work or home number. Meet him at a mutually agreed upon <u>public</u> location. Until you get to know and trust him, you need to keep yourself safe.

Be honest with yourself. Being honest makes it easier to be straightforward with the other person. Let him know, "I am interested in going out with you, getting to know you, but if we don't hit it off, we can just be friends or move on." Be upfront.

You like what you like. Be true to what you like. You do not have to make excuses for what you like. If you like a man that dresses a certain way, or has a certain look, or if his income bracket or social status matters to you – **be true to yourself**. Do not sell yourself short. If you are not attracted to him, do not settle.

Use common sense. Some people just do not take rejection well, or may become provoked by you calling it quits and abruptly ending the relationship. (This is another reason why you should guard your personal information.) If you sense this is the type of man you are dating, you need to be **wise**. You may need to walk softly, to break it off gently. You want to try to make it seem that it is you, and not him. "You are a really great guy, but I'm not ready for a relationship." "I'm currently seeing someone else." "I'm not really looking for a relationship right now, but a friendship. I need to get myself together."

<u>Listen closely</u>. Sometimes he will give you a way out. He might say that he does not like a par-

ticular thing, or that he is looking for a specific type of relationship. If that occurs it, is easier for you to tell him; "Wow, I'm just the opposite." Still make it seem that it is you who is not ready, but try to use what he says so that <u>he</u> will end it.

Accept rejection. If he does not want to see you again, move on. It was only a date. You two did not connect. Even if you believe there was a connection, if he is not interested, he will make it known. Avoidance is a clear indicator of lack of interest. Do not deceive yourself into believing there is more to the relationship when you are getting the brush-off.

Chapter 2: Sex on the First Date

Call it what you will; a One-Night Stand, Hooking-Up, Booty-Call, Knocking Boots, Boning, a Quick-Fix, Getting Laid, a Fast Lay, a Roll in the Hay, you Hit It and Quit It, but you are having sex with a man you just met! It is extremely rare that a man will say, "No, don't have sex with me!" if you are willing to put-out on the first date. Ultimately, it is his goal to have sex with you, so sex on the first date fits right into his agenda.

I spoke to many women and only a few developed a long-term relationship with a man they have had sex with on the first date. Most women shared with me that it was their only date and they received the brush-off, or if there was a second date, which also led to sex, then they received the brush-off, or that the relationship remained sexual and they only hooked-up with the guy when either party wanted sex. None of these "dates" developed into meaningful relationships. In fact, the women shared that they often felt pain, regret, and even a sense of loss associated with these one-time experiences.

Of the men I spoke with, most of them confirmed that they have given the brush-off to women who slept with them on the first or even the second date. Many of the men shared that they really did not foresee a long-term relationship with a woman who gave them sex after first meeting them.

The consensus was that the men had trust issues, which may sound hypocritical, but the men felt that if a woman could so easily have sex with them, and they just met, then the assumption is that she could and would easily have sex with the next man. In addition, they did not want to bring a woman home as a girlfriend or a wife if they perceived her as a "freak." A "freak" is slang for a woman or man known to be promiscuous, <u>and</u> willing to engage in illicit, explicit, or deviant sexual acts. Let's face it, "why (should they) buy the cow when they can get the milk for free?"

The truth of the matter is that men like promiscuous women in bed; they are great sex partners. However, although they may want a freak in bed, they do not want to marry a freak; OR they want a freak, but they do not want her to be <u>obvious</u>. Moreover, they fear that same promiscuity when it comes to their personal ideals of who a woman should be in a committed relationship. Whereas, they may desire their wife to be sexy, they <u>do</u> <u>not</u> want her to be a "Ho." **A man typically wants a woman that he can respect and trust.**

Do not have sex on the first date. Give yourself the opportunity to get to know the man. He may be a good guy or he may be a nut. You want to know who he is, what kind of man he is, and WHAT HIS SEXUAL HISTORY IS before you are intimate with him.

Once you sleep with him, you cannot take it back. You cannot go back and change what you have done. By having sex with him on the first or second date, he may perceive you to be easy, a slut, or a freak. You develop a reputation that, once it is known, other men will want to "date" you so that they too can have you. Be aware that men talk, so they know who is easy, and who is not.

Do not place yourself in a compromising situation. Your first date should not be dinner at his house, or your home, for that matter. Similarly, why <u>are</u> you at his house or apartment after your date, or vice versa? Use wisdom and set Godly boundaries.

- Set a time limit for your date. Give yourself a reason to be home by a reasonable hour. Instead of going on a dinner date, have lunch or meet for coffee.

- Do not drink alcohol. Alcohol can impair your thinking, and can inhibit your ability to make sound decisions.

- Do not drink from a cup you cannot "see." If the drink is not poured in front of you, if the bottle is already opened, if a glass is "offered" to you, or if you turn your back or walk away from your glass, DO NOT DRINK IT! Even if you've asked someone to monitor your drink, **YOU DO NOT KNOW IF THE "DATE RAPE" DRUG WAS SLIPPED INTO YOUR DRINK** when you were not looking.

- Do not provide him with too much information. He does not need to know how enamored you are with him, or that you have a crush on him. Additionally, he should not know that your roommate or parent(s) is out of town, and that you essentially, have no one to serve as a buffer, or as protection.

- Do not invite someone you do not know into your home or naively go into his. The mere fact that you have invited him over or that you go back to his place might lead him to believe that you will have, or want to have sex with him. **Moreover, even if you say "NO," he might not stop.**

- Do not allow his words to cause you to give up the "goods". It does not matter what he says, how smoothly or suggestively he says them, stick to your guns. YOU DO NOT KNOW THIS MAN. Do not allow him to coax you into a decision you will later regret. He may act indignant and say, "I can't believe you won't have sex with me;" or he may suggest that you want to, by saying "You know you want it." He might even threaten to never see you again. **Stand by your decision,** cut your losses and move on. He is obviously not the man for you.

- **NEVER, EVER, EVER HAVE UNPROTECTED SEX!!**
  Having unprotected sex is equivalent to playing Russian roulette. You are not only sleeping with your current partner, but every partner he has <u>ever</u> slept with, and every partner they have <u>ever</u> slept with, and so on, and so forth. Additionally, the risks are high, serious, and can be deadly.

  Besides pregnancy, you can contract a host of sexual transmitted diseases (STDs). STDs are infections that you can get from having sex with someone who has the infection. The causes of STDs are bacteria, parasites and viruses, many of which are transmitted via blood, saliva, semen, or vaginal secretions. There are more than 20 types of STDs, including Chlamydia, Gonorrhea, Herpes Simplex, HPV and Genital Warts, Syphilis, Trichomoniasis, Hepatitis, Pubic Lice (Crabs), HIV/AIDS. **Having unprotected sex can be a death sentence.**

- Know <u>your</u> limits. If kissing turns you on, or opens the door to intimacy, do not kiss him on your date. Do not allow him to grind on you, touch you intimately or suggestively. If sitting in the car late hours under moonlight turns your date into "Denzel or Brad Pitt", then do not linger. Say thank you and goodbye.

You want to keep a man motivated. The pursuit is a challenge to men. Once he has sex with you, there is no challenge, and the hunt is over. His interest wanes, because not only did he get what he came for, but also by becoming intimate with him so quickly, he did not even have to work for it. Once he has "had" you, he will just move on. If your goal is to develop a long-term relationship with him, do not have sex with him. (Make him) wait.

Create standards and stick by them. He needs to be more into you than you are into him. He must know that you are the prize. <u>You</u> must know that you are the prize. Sex on the first date, does not a prize make. You will only be treated as well as you require a man to treat you.

Additionally, **set the bar high enough**. A man will only jump as high as he needs to. Therefore, if your standards or expectations are too low, he will not attempt to exceed those expectations. With sex on the first date, you set the bar low enough for him to walk right over it, and you.

One thing <u>does</u> <u>not</u> lead to another. There is a time in the "heat of the moment," that you <u>think</u> and make a conscious decision to keep going or to stop. Saying "one thing led to another" is a poor excuse. Exercise self-control. The passion is never so great, neither are you so overcome with pleasure that you cannot think. Instead, you ignore the voice, the reason. Passion may cloud your judgment, but the choice is still yours. <u>One thing can only lead to another, when you let it</u>.

When you wait, you make better choices. Time is a beautiful thing. With time, you are able to obtain a more complete picture of the man you are dating, the person you are getting to know. When you wait, you are able to make smarter decisions, because you do not allow pressure to influence you, cause you to act hastily or make a decision you may later regret. **In life, the very thing**

you cannot live without today, you find is **the** **thing you can live without it tomorrow.**

Respect yourself. Understand that you are worth getting to know. Let him put the time and effort into getting to know you by actually dating you. Do not make it so easy for him that he loses his interest in or his respect for you. If he cannot wait, or gives you the brush-off, date someone else. HE OBVIOUSLY IS NOT THE MAN FOR YOU.

What kind of "ride" are you? When you buy a car, you can either go to the Mercedes Benz dealer, or to the used car lot. In order to buy a top of the line car, you must be credit worthy, you must present yourself well, and you must prove that you are capable of purchasing a car of high caliber. The salesperson treats you with a certain level of respect. Whereas, when you go to the used car lot, image is not as important. The standards for vehicle purchase are lower. The dealership may even overlook your credit worthiness.

There is a reason why a Mercedes Benz is valued high. The creators of the Benz use top of the line products; they took their time choosing materials. From the interior to the exterior, the car is made to meet the specifications and quality that people come to expect. Whereas, at the used car lot, your expectations are lower. In essence, you get what you pay for. KNOW YOUR VALUE! Do you see yourself as a luxury car, or as a used car? **How we value ourselves oftentimes, dictate how others will value us.**

There is an expression that we use to say in college, "What's worth having is worth waiting for," and

You Are Worth It!

Chapter 3: Long-Term Commitment

There is a point where dating evolves into a long-term relationship. You have been dating, and at this point, you have developed a genuine friendship. You both decide to commit to one another exclusively. Maybe he is tired of starting over, or he is ready to settle down, get married and have children, but your objective is to be together for an extended time. It is a stage in the relationship when you know that you are in love and make an effort to make the relationship work.

You trust him enough to put time into the relationship. People around you (family, friends, co-workers, etc.) <u>know</u> that you two are a couple, and, hopefully, support the endeavor.

Communication is the key. A sense of mutual understanding and sympathy must exist. Are you able to express your ideas or feelings freely? Are you willing to <u>listen</u> even if you strongly disagree? Are you capable of being honest and straightforward while having regard for his feelings? Can you receive criticism, or are you easily offended? Loving someone is great, but it is the daily communications that determines the success of your relationship.

- Be open and honest. Learn to talk things through. Even if what he does annoys you, and he will annoy you, talk about it. Do not let negative emotions build.

- Be a person of your word. Your word is your bond. If you say you're going to do something, do it. Moreover, if you are unable to do what you have stated, do not act as if you have never said it. Acknowledge the fact that you said it, but let him know you are unable to perform the task. If you act as if you have never said it, he will not trust your word.

- Be a person of integrity, veracity, and trustworthiness. Be that person he knows is upright; one he can trust to do what is right, to make the right choices in a situation and in life.

- Respect his boundaries. Communication will help you understand each other's boundaries – what your mate will tolerate; understanding when he needs his space, what irks him, or which of his papers you cannot touch or move.

- Communication will help you maintain your friendship.

Discuss long-term goals. Is he looking for a committed relationship? Are you two on the same page in terms of your expectations and goals? Do you both expect the same outcome for your relationship? Does he want to get married, want children, or is he just looking for a committed relationship without marriage, or children?

Discuss Finances. Are you going to combine finances, keep them separate, or a combination of the two? Do you have the same expectations about money and future financial goals? Do you know who is better at managing money? **FINANCIAL STRAIN WILL CAUSE THE RELATIONSHIP TO END.**

Be willing to compromise. You cannot have everything your way. There has to be give and take. Be willing to learn to concede, yield, cease opposing one another and come to an agreement.

Many times you will not compromise because of pride or because you do not want to admit that you are wrong. Pride can be detrimental to your relationship. It causes you to make foolish decisions, to be obstinate and inflexible, to behave like a jerk, or to hold fast to your point of view, even when you are dead wrong. Pride can alienate you from your mate.

Choose your battles. Not every provocation warrants a battle. Not every conversation warrants a fight. Take off your boxing gloves, and do not allow your actions to provoke the fight. For example, do not slam his food on the plate and then slam his plate on the table. Take a deep breath…not every argument warrants a knock-down-drag-out fight.

Choose wisely. Don't sweat the small stuff. Even if something bothers you, some things are just not worth arguing about especially when conceding is beneficial to the relationship. Sometimes you just need to let it go and the opportunity to discuss it rationally will present itself later.

Be willing to humble yourself. You do not always have to be right. You do not always have to prove that you are his equal. You cannot butt heads in every situation. You must be willing to relent. Not every situation warrants a response, a confrontation, or a contest of wills. Your tongue is a very powerful weapon. It can build a person up, or it will tear someone down. Sometimes you have to concede, to surrender, to yield, to let it go, to learn <u>not</u> to argue back. Humility allows you to defer to his knowledge, his judgment, and his experience. Humility makes it possible for you to admit when you are wrong. Humility also makes it probable that you will submit.

Get a grip on your emotions. Women can be very emotional. Expressing emotion is part of a woman's make-up but there has to be a balance. It is unhealthy to be overly emotional. It is unwise to allow your emotions to rule your life. You cannot make every decision based on your emotions. Being emotional clouds your judgment and being emotional causes others to characterize you as unstable.

Be reasonable. When your emotions are controlling you, you are unable to think clearly and sensibly, and you may be incapable of making rational judgments. No one wants to be in a relationship with a nut!

Know how to be vulnerable. Know how to express emotion, to communicate your feelings, to let him know when you are crying, and if you are hurt or upset. Although you may have been deeply hurt in a past relationship, you cannot allow that hurt to prevent you from opening up in your current relationship. You cannot be as hard as a man.

A man wants a woman to be a woman; to be feminine, to show emotion, and to convey softness. It is okay to be intelligent, self-sufficient, and independent, but it is not conducive to your relationship to act as if you do not "need" or want a man. A MAN WANTS TO KNOW THAT HE IS BOTH NEEDED AND WANTED. A man may provide for you, he may provide for his family, which fulfills a need. If he does not believe or feel that you want him, then he may look outside of the relationship for someone who does. A man knows when this is part of your make-up, your beliefs, and **HE WILL NOT WANT TO STAY IN A RELATIONSHIP WITH YOU IF YOU DO NOT NEED OR WANT HIM**.

Do not be so quick to catch an attitude, to allow every little thing to make you angry. Constantly being angry or having an attitude will blind you from the truth, and hinder you from working things out with your mate. Anger or attitude can make you combative and contentious. Such behavior may also cause others to characterize you as a moody person, or a dour person, meaning a person who is never happy, or satisfied. People might think you are a sourpuss; a person who is just plain ole' mean and nasty. Learn how to disagree without being disagreeable.

Do not be easily offended. Do not take offense to every word. Some things are not said to offend you or to intentionally hurt you. Some things you need to let roll off you like the water off a duck's back. You do not want him to feel as if he has to walk on eggshells around you, or that he has to re-think or rehearse every word he utters to you. **TAKING OFFENSE TO EVERY LITTLE THING HE SAYS OR DOES WILL EVENTUALLY STIFLE COMMUNICATION, AND ULTIMATELY STRAIN THE RELATIONSHIP.**

Nip it in the bud. <u>And</u> if you <u>are</u> offended or hurt by what he says, express it, deal with it, and move on. Do not let the offense build, do not hold a grudge, and do not let his actions get to a point where the first time he is hearing about the offense is when you explode. Be fair in your communication, because he might not know what the offense is. Give him the opportunity to make it right.

Do not be a Nag. <u>NO ONE</u> wants to be nagged, to be constantly reminded of something, or repeatedly asked and harassed about a situation. No man wants to be criticized, hen-pecked, or nit-picked. **NAGGING GETS OLD VERY QUICKLY, AND WILL CAUSE AN END TO YOUR RELATIONSHIP.**

Do not expect him to jump, because you say jump. Do not expect a thing to be done, exactly when <u>you</u> want it done. Instead of nagging, let him know what you would like done, and give him a reasonable time frame to complete the task. Try asking, "Baby, do you think you can get the dishes washed before we go to bed?"

Do not direct. Do not micromanage. Do not stand over his shoulder and direct all of his actions. Give him room to make his own decisions and give him room to breathe. If he takes it upon himself to tackle an activity or to fix a situation, let him do it without you being the armchair quarterback, or the backseat driver. If you ask him to take care of a matter for you, do not give him a play-by-play analysis of how you think it should be done, even when you believe it is warranted. Especially when he gives you that "look" – back off! IF HE DOES NOT ASK YOU, DO NOT SUPERVISE! HE IS NOT A CHILD! **UNWANTED ADVICE OR UNSOLICITED SUPERVISION MAY ULTIMATELY CAUSE HIM TO RESENT YOU.**

Avoid power tripping. Stop trying to manipulate the situation, or manipulate him so that you have the upper hand or to prove that you are in control. If it is not your goal to make him feel like he is less than a man, then stop trying to show him who is boss. Similarly, if you do not like to be belittled, do not belittle him.

Avoid vain arguments. Most arguments are one-sided, so why waste your time and energy arguing when the other party either is not listening or does not hear you. Unless you raise a question to solicit an answer people will tune you out. In most instances, they do not listen. In other words, you have to ask a question, you must be seeking an answer, or provoke a question to get an answer. For example, when you ask, "Do you understand what I am saying?" you are asking a question. If a person is not asked a question, he will never give you an answer, so you are just venting, and your argument is in vain.

Listen! Pay attention to what he says. Sometimes he will verbalize how he feels. Other times, there are only non-verbal cues. A big part of healthy communication is the ability to listen. Hear him out.

Do not make light of, downplay, underemphasize, or treat what he is trying to say as insignificant. Do not try to anticipate what he is going to say, finish his sentences for him, or calculate your response while he is still speaking. Do not zone out or tune him out even when he is repeating the same thing, over and over again. You will not only miss something he is trying to share with you or tell you, but you risk frustrating him because he never gets the chance to express himself. Moreover, when you fail to listen, you miss what he <u>means</u>; More damagingly, you risk shutting down communication, and he might stop trying to share his feelings or thoughts with you, completely. **FAILURE TO LISTEN STRAINS COMMUNICATION.**

Additionally, do not be so quick to take the defensive, to make excuses, or to rationalize and justify what he is saying to you. When you are constantly defensive, or are quick to make excuses, it gives off the impression that you are automatically <u>rejecting</u> what is being said to you, because you cannot hear him. Therefore, if his point is valid – you have missed it.

Life is <u>not</u> a television show. You learn about relationships and love from television – sitcoms, talk shows, or movies, and then try to apply or incorporate what you have seen and heard into your personal experiences. When your situation does not play out the way it occurs on TV, or the way you imagined it should, you are baffled. Remember, sitcoms, movies, and even talk shows are well scripted and rehearsed. Paid professionals write the beginning, the middle and all of the outcomes. LIFE IS <u>NEVER</u> WELL SCRIPTED! BE PREPARED FOR REALITY.

Be willing to forgive. He is going to make you angry; he will get under your skin, and he will work your last nerve. He will upset you, and he may hurt your feelings. You must learn to forgive and let it go. Do not hold a grudge. Communicate your feelings, work it out and do not hold on to it. **FAILURE TO FORGIVE CREATES BARRIERS**

AND ULTIMATELY DETERIORATES YOUR RELATIONSHIP.

Accept the unexpected. How do you handle the unexpected? Even if you have plotted out every aspect of your life, even if you have a contingency plan for your contingency plan, there will be unexpected circumstances that arise, and unplanned events that will affect your relationship. How you handle these situations is crucial to the longevity of your relationship. Can you move forward from these events? Either you will work through it, work it out, and come to a mutual understanding, or these trials and events will separate you.

Be willing to grow, to become a better person for one another. Continue to work on your character, to be upright, to be the best person you can be. Be willing to move forward. You must be flexible and able to adapt to change or at the very least, be open to change according to the circumstances. Do not be so rigid, or set in your ways, that you stifle your relationship by your obstinacy and lack of flexibility.

Recognize <u>yourself</u> in the relationship. Who you are, what kind of person you are in the relationship. Are you selfish and self-centered? Are you jealous and possessive? On the other hand, are you loving, do you show affection, are you supportive? Do not only focus on his flaws while ignoring, denying, or blinding yourself to your own. By recognizing who you are, you will not only be able to confront your own issues as they arise, but be prepared to deal with them, and grow.

Do not take him for granted. Love him for who he is. Do not be so comfortable that you do not take his feelings, his wants or his needs into consideration. Appreciate the things he does, no matter how small, and <u>show</u> <u>it</u>. Let him know that you appreciate him. Do not abuse his kindness, or take his kindness for weakness.

Do not try to change him; people do not change simply because you want them to – what you see is what you get. Accept him for who he is. If you cannot accept him, then why continue in a relationship with him?

It is the little things that make a person happy. If it is a minor thing, and you <u>know</u> it makes your mate happy, then do it even if it is not a part of your personality. For example, acknowledge your mate when he calls or texts, write a love note, or give a card if you know he finds that sort of thing romantic.

If you give of yourself freely, selflessly, and he does the same, then you both have each other's best interest at heart, which is an ideal situation.

Do not change who you are, now that you have gotten him. Continue to do those things you did to get him. If he likes romance, continue to be romantic. If he likes a home-cooked meal, continue to cook for him, occasionally.

Men like what they like. Whatever it is that makes you attractive to him, he expects that thing to remain the same. Do not be surprised if he cannot deal with a dramatic change. He may be able to handle you enhancing what he already likes. However, if you do not like you and work to change you, he may not like it; even though you are doing what you believe is best for you.

For example, you were a dependent woman when you met him, and you decide that you will no longer be dependent, so you become independent. You were at a weight he desired when you met and you either gain or lose substantial weight. As a result, the attraction for you is no longer there because he liked the person you were when you entered the relationship. That is, the thing that attracted him to you has changed; you have changed, and he no longer desires you. **DRAMATIC CHANGES WILL CAUSE A STRAIN TO YOUR RELATIONSHIP.**

Do not be surprised if he does not marry you, when you do everything a wife would do. Do you cook for him? Clean up after him, do his laundry? Do you live with him, sleep with him? Do you want him to marry you? Why does he need to marry you, when you do everything a wife does without his commitment? He has no incentive, no vows to keep, no sense of obligation, when he is getting all of the benefits of marriage without being married.

Find out where he stands. Stop doing those things that a wife does. Stop sleeping with him; stop fulfilling all of his needs. You will quickly find out where you stand. He will make the commitment, he will make excuses, or you will be out the door.

Do not embarrass him. Do not cause him to feel inadequate or inferior. Do not humiliate him or make him feel less than a man, especially in public or when others are present. A man never wants to feel emasculated, or appear weak. No man wants to be antagonized, treated or spoken to in a condescending manner. Embarrassment bruises his ego, causes frustration, and triggers his pride.

Also, do what is appropriate – do what is suitable for the circumstances. Do not make him look bad; do not make yourself look bad. Act appropriately. Wear what is appropriate. For example, if you are 40, do not dress as if you are 16. Know how to represent.

Do not make him feel stupid. Men do not like to feel stupid. Do not make him feel less than adequate, like he is not as smart as you are. Even if you are smarter, do not condescend, or talk down to him; do not make him feel like he does not measure-up.

Do not disrespect him. Do not speak to him as if you are the parent and he the child. Do not lay him out, tell him off, and argue with him in front of your children, your friends, the family, in public. Do not make major or life-altering decisions without consulting him.

Do not stare at other men when you are in his presence. Do not hug-up, be overly affectionate toward another man, or show undue interest. If that person is not your brother, or a family member, then your mate will deem your abundance of affection as inappropriate. In addition, a man feels disrespected when he asks or tells you not to do a certain thing and you do that very thing.

Let a man be a man. He had friends before he met you. Allow him to hang out with his buddies, to go out with his male friends. Let him have his space, his time away from you. Similarly, you do not want him to go to the nail or beauty salon with you, do you?

Avoid bringing baggage from past relationships into your current relationship. Do not audibly compare him to past boyfriends. Do not keep telling him that he reminds you of your ex, or that he does something just like your ex. Not only does this show a lack of maturity, but also it will cause him to believe that you still have feelings for your ex.

You probably will mentally compare him to others anyway – this is human nature. The comparison often serves as a warning, especially when you identify behavior that you have dealt with in the past. HOWEVER, HE DOES NOT WANT TO

HEAR IT! In his mind, if he is so much like your ex, why did you not <u>stay</u> with your ex?

Another issue women bring from past relationships is lack of trust. This does not mean disregard common sense, but if he has earned your trust, give it to him.

Do not talk about past sexual experiences. He really <u>does not</u> want to hear about your promiscuity, sexual conquests, or your sex acts with other men. Call it possessiveness, call it ego, call it old-fashioned, or call it what you will, but he does not want to be reminded that you have had sex with other men. Remember, he does not want to believe that his girlfriend, or his wife, that the person that he is in a committed relationship with, has been a "freak"; he does not want to be reminded that he is with a woman who has been entered by multiple men.

Even If you feel <u>compelled</u> to be honest, a lot of men cannot handle <u>knowing</u> your past sexual exploits. Sharing this kind of information can backfire. He may pull away, he may want to end the relationship, or he may later throw what you have told him into your face by reminding you of what "kind" of woman you were. It may cause him to mistrust you, or lose respect for you. There really is a different standard for women than there is for men.

Do not betray his trust. Trust is a tenuous emotion. It is fragile, and can easily be broken. Because of the baggage that people have in their lives, trust is an entity that is difficult to earn, but more significantly, it is a privilege that is even more difficult to regain, if lost.
A LACK OF TRUST WILL CAUSE COMMUNICATION TO DETERIORATE AND WILL KILL YOUR RELATIONSHIP.

Stay Focused! Stay on track. If your goal is to be in a committed relationship, focus on your relationship; focus on your mate. Put in the time and energy needed to make it work. Do not become distracted by other men you meet. The grass is not always greener on the other side.

The grass is <u>NOT</u> always greener... Do not covet your neighbor's grass. Your neighbor's grass may look beautiful, lush, alive, attractive, fertile, and almost perfect, but have you considered the labor involved to make that grass look so green? What does it take to grow greener grass? – raking, seeding, tilling, planting, fertilizing, weeding, watering, tending, caring, manicuring, nurturing, and de-bugging. Your neighbor not only had to cultivate that lawn to make it look so green, but also must continue to maintain and nurture it to keep it healthy.

Additionally, take a closer look at your neighbor's grass. Is it really so green, or are there some yellow patches still? If you would take the time to sow your own lawn, that is sow into your relationship, then your grass would be as green too.

> Thou shalt not covet thy neighbour's house, thou shalt not covet thy neighbour's wife, nor his manservant, nor his maidservant, nor his ox, nor his ass, nor any thing that is thy neighbour's.
> (Exodus 20:17, KJV)

Do not be so quick to give up. There will be bumps in the road. There will be surprises. There will be trials. Relationships require fortitude, perseverance, a willingness to stick it out during the tough times. TOUGH IT OUT! You must take the bitter with the sweet. Your relationship will not always be smooth sailing. There will be situations that are difficult and painful, and circumstances that require strength, endurance, faith, courage, and resolve. If you <u>both</u> are determined to have your relationship succeed, you can make it through these times.

Make a commitment to make the relationship work and resolve to be <u>happy</u> in your relationship.

He Loves You, Not

Chapter 4: Trust Your Gut

Have you ever been out with someone and you get a feeling that he is not the person for you? Have you ever met that someone who looked good from afar, but was far from good? Let me qualify this statement. There really are some good men out there. There are those who are sincere; they are seeking a committed relationship. They dress well, have a job, and are stable. There are men who even love the Lord and who treat you well. There are also men that were hurt, and therefore, can make a lousy first impression. And there are some people with whom you just do not hit it off. Nevertheless, there is that circumstance where you know something is not right.

Sometimes that feeling comes with flashing red lights, bells, and whistles. He manifests violent tendencies, is quick tempered, or behaves irrationally. He may be extremely possessive, controlling, or he may react in a way that turns you off. He is a man that you, without any doubt, will not date again.

Have you met these men?

- **The Sly-talker**: The man who makes you feel good with words. He has the gift of gab. He knows how to manipulate words to get what he wants. His words are oily like melted butter. (His motive is to get you into bed).

- **The Future Stalker**: The man who checks in on you every once and a while; he keeps tabs on you and he does not take rejection well. He is possessive and controlling, and he always seems to be plotting his next move.

- **The Stalker**: The man who watches you in a threatening and/or menacing manner. He is aware of your every move. If you date him, he will never let you go, although you are dating someone else.

- **The Potential Wife-beater**: Jealous, extremely possessive, intimidating and can be verbally, mentally, or physically abusive.

- **Mr. Materialistic**: He keeps tabs on the gifts he gives you, so that he can hang his "generosity" over your head when it is convenient for him. His expectation is that since he is your "Sugar Daddy," you belong to him.

- **The Pretty Boy**: He looks out for himself, he takes care of himself, he looks better than a woman does, and he causes you to wonder about his heterosexuality.

- **Mr. It's-All-About-Him**: The world revolves around him. He is self-absorbed. His entire conversation is about himself. From his expensive car, his job, his hairstylist, to who does his nails, even why he picked the wine. You do not get a word in edgewise.

    He is not merely selfish and self-centered, he is so programmed that you have to fit into his lifestyle. You are not there to share his life – you too are scheduled in. At the end of the evening, he has a good time and you just smile and nod, because it is all about him.

- **The Adulterer**: He presents himself as single, when he is not, and therefore, he is capable of having more than one "family." That is, he has a wife and child(ren) in one place, and a girlfriend and child in another place...Or he strings you along by telling you he is separated or in the process of a divorce. However, he will <u>never</u> leave his wife, whom he loves.

- **The "Wolf in Sheep's Clothing"**: He appears to be a Godly man. He looks pious, and you would think he was the most saved person in the church. However, he is the man that uses the church to pick-up or hit-on women.

    He is very observant and is keenly aware of your comings and goings. He talks to you, is very friendly with you, and can be extremely complimentary. He is the man who grabs your hand and rubs your fingers, or if he kisses your cheek, he misses and hits your lips. He woos you with the Word of God, while he seduces you with his actions. His goal is to sift you like wheat – to separate you, to cause you to compromise. These men know their prey, and prey on your weakness. Like vultures, they ease in quietly, they get what they came for, and leave before they are caught.

- **The Deflector**: He is constantly accusing you of indiscretion or cheating without provocation or merit. The very fact that he is asking you, "Are you having an affair?" or "Are you seeing someone else?" is the art of deflection. He deflects because he is more than likely doing the very thing he is accusing you of, or at least contemplating committing the act; he may even be feeling guilty.

  He shifts the focus on to you in order to minimize his own actions and indiscretions. For example, he questions your every move, asks whom are you talking to on the phone; he answers the phone for you, or places the call on speaker so that he will know who it is. He questions your whereabouts and wants to know the time you are coming home, so that he can do his dirty without being caught. He deflects to draw attention away from himself, so that you will not see what he is doing.

He will cause you to fall into his web of deceit. In response, you begin to curb your behavior, limit your interactions with friends, family or co-workers, and terminate any outside activities that do not involve him. His interrogations will have you monitoring your own actions instead of his.

- **The "Friend"**: He appears eager to listen to your relationship woes, yet he uses your vulnerability to get you into bed.

- **The Counterfeit**: He appears to be genuine. He appears to be the man for you. He possesses all of the qualities you like, want, and look for in a man. You two hit it off, you get along, and you are compatible. It appears that the relationship is progressing; you even are in agreement about future goals. However, he is not the real thing. He is the man who leads you on, but will not commit.

- **Mr. Waiting in the Wings**: He is always there; he is always standing by. He is friendly with you, with your mate, your spouse, so that he <u>knows</u> about your relationship. He watches your relationship, waiting for it to fail, waiting for you to <u>need</u> him. He is the person who offers, "You know I'm here for you, if you need me." He is deceptive; he is opportunistic; he is the snake in the grass waiting to strike, waiting for a sexual relationship with you. He derives a sense of joy, of pride from the conquest, <u>and</u> he keeps score.

- **The Lecher**: He behaves lewdly and lustfully, to the degree that it is distasteful and inappropriate. He will hit on you at a funeral. Before the body is even in the grave, he will put his bid in for your affection. "You know I am here for you if you need me…" He is the man that "accidently" bumps up against you or grinds on you with a hard-on, or suggests you sit on his lap, so that he can cop a feel. He is vulgar and obscene and finds it humorous to be offensive. He has an attraction to young flesh, and will often try to 'screw' or 'score' with anyone who has a youthful appearance. He epitomizes the expression 'dirty old man.'

- **The "Secret Boyfriend"**: He is your man, and you two are in a relationship, but NO ONE ELSE KNOWS ABOUT IT! He has never introduced you to his friends or his family, nor does he intend to. It is his idea to keep your relationship a secret, because he is seeing someone else and you are the only one who does not know it, or who does not <u>want</u> to know it.

- **Mr. I Got It Like That**: He dresses well, smells good, has a good job and has assets; he is attractive, and he <u>knows</u> it.

- **Mr. "Showcase"**: You are a showpiece, a trophy. He pays for your hair appointments, your nails; he picks out your clothes. He presents you in a way designed to attract attention and admiration. You are on display. This gives him a sense of self-satisfaction. He expects you to match his image and he will dump you if your image changes, or if he perceives that you have changed. You must meet his ideal of the perfect woman.

- **The Octopus**: He is touchy – feely. He cannot keep his hands off you; he cannot keep his hands to himself. His hands are so quick, it seems like he has eight of them. Once you are in his tentacles, you cannot escape. He wants to touch you all over the place; you cannot seem to get out of his grasp. He expresses himself by squeezing your shoulder, rubbing or squeezing your thigh. His advances toward you are creepy and slimy.

- **The Perfectionist**: He demonstrates obsessive-compulsive behavior. Nothing can be out of place. He dresses impeccably, is a neat freak and is bound by a schedule. <u>Nothing</u> in his world can be out of place, not even you.

- **The Flirt**: He undresses you with his eyes. He makes his actions seem innocent or innocuous, but they are actually a mechanism or ploy to get you into bed. He fills his conversations with sexual innuendoes. Be aware that he is flirtatious with every woman that he meets.

- **Mr. Conceited**: He is vain; vanity run-amok. He is arrogant and self-serving.

- **The Intellectual**: Very intelligent, highly-educated, usually a professional. He is never wrong and even when he is, he will not admit it.

    He is very impressed with himself, and he expects others to be equally, or more impressed. He is so impressed with his credentials that he feels no reservations, no shame about singing his own praises.

    He is logical, practical, and has the tendency to over-analyze every decision, every circumstance, which limits his willingness to take risks. He does not like to feel that a situation is out of control, and will avoid placing himself in a position beyond his control. Because of his practicality, his level-headedness, his need to stay in control, he truly lacks emotion.

- **Mr. Insecure**: He cannot bear a woman making more money than he does, or he is constantly accusing you of cheating on him.

- **The Constant Talker**: He is a know-it-all. He will not shut-up! He is boastful, full of himself, and he <u>knows</u> <u>EVERYTHING</u>!

- **The Habitual Liar**: He begins to stu-stutter when explaining his actions; his story constantly changes; or he is good at lying, but after awhile, the pieces do not add up.

- **The Faker**: He is good at deception. He dresses well and talks a good game, but in reality, he is a bum. He has no ambition, no motivation, and no goals, except to have you take care of him, of course. (He probably still lives with his mother.)

- **The Taker**: This is the man who will take anything you have to give, and all you can give. He will take up your time, he will spend your money, he will deplete your resources and your assets; he will deplete your energy; he will take advantage of you. There is no give and take. He just takes, and takes, and takes, until you have nothing left to give. Then once he has taken all you have, you are left with nothing, and he moves on.

- **The Derelict**: He is a bum; he is neglectful of his duties, of his obligations and responsibilities. He will not keep a job; he will not try or will only make half-hearted attempts to find employment. He lacks moral balance, a sense of propriety – a sense of rightness; he does not possess any guilt or regret for his inactivity. He is living the good life, and is comfortable with sitting on the couch while his woman supports him.

- **The "Goal" Digger:** He has goals; he has dreams. He needs you to accomplish these goals. He needs your resources and your resourcefulness. He needs you to keep his house in order, his life in order. He stands on your back while he attains his goals. You are his support, his cheerleader, the person who takes up the slack.

   Whether he is trying to achieve a degree, or a position at work, you stand by him through the exams, the papers, the finals, the promotions, through the stress. Unfortunately, when he accomplishes his goal, when he reaches his finish line, he no longer has a place for you. He no longer wants you or needs you – you do not meet his standards.

- **The Great Pretender**: He "acts" as if he is the man for you. He is impressive, he is attentive, he does all the things you like; he takes you out and he is a wonderful person that you fall in love with. However, once he has you, he stops doing the things you like. He no longer tries to impress you; he stops being attentive. He stops taking you out and he avoids or makes excuses for doing things, which he knows makes you happy.

He appears to be a different person when, in fact, he has never changed. He has been playing a role. He was just manipulating you to get you, and now that he has you, he no longer will hide whom he truly is.

- **Not "Prince Charming," he is just a Frog**: How many frogs have you come across in your life? You think you have found prince charming, but he is just another frog in disguise. You want to believe he is the one. He looks the part, he dresses the part, he may even act the part, initially, but soon you discover he is a toad. Maybe, he is an emerging prince – a frog in transformation, but no matter how many times you kiss him he never becomes a prince; he is just a frog.

- **The Beggar**: He never seems to have or keep any money. He regularly asks you to lend him a few dollars, with the promise to repay you. Nevertheless, he feels no accountability. Even if he gives you a few bucks as repayment, it is only to appease you, so that he can borrow from you again. He really believes he is not obligated to pay you back, nor does he feel any responsibility towards your possessions.

He will borrow your car; he will borrow your credit – if you let him. If he crashes your car, you wind up paying for the repairs; if he runs up your credit, you pay to repair that too. He will never repay you everything you have lent him. You ultimately are stuck footing the bill.

- **Player, Playaah**: He is a womanizer. He objectifies women. He uses women just for the sex, and what they can do for him. He is skilled at manipulating ("playing") women, and especially at seducing women by pretending to care about them, when in reality he is only interested in the sex. He is usually well taken care of by women (I use the plural intentionally); consequently, he has no interest in commitment, loyalty, or love.

- **The Dog**: He is a man who hits and runs, that is, he tells women what they want to hear to get into their panties, and as soon as he gets the goods, he is gone. He is unwilling or unable to commit to one woman.

- **Mr. 8 to 80**: He will date you from age eight to age eighty, sane or crazy. He will date, hence, sleep with, anything that moves. He lacks discretion, because in his mind sex has no face. That is, it does not matter who you are, what you look like, or what your issues are, he just wants to get laid.

- **"Baby Daddy"**: He will not be a <u>father</u> to his children. He will not take care of his responsibility and you have to take him to court for child support. Either he is controlling, whereas no one can mind the child except for the mother, or he keeps the child a secret and will not be daddy to the child publicly.

He becomes Mr. Do Drop In. He drops in for a short time and then he has to leave, or he makes a date to see his kid(s), but then he does not show up, as promised. Essentially, the mother is a single parent. He usually is "Baby Daddy" to a number of children.

- **Mr. Military**: He has the freedom to travel, so he may have a "relationship" with you, but be aware that he is more likely than not, in a "relationship" with another woman somewhere else.

Sometimes there are no sirens, bells or whistles. It is really just a feeling that something is not right. It may be a sensation so brief that you almost can convince yourself that what you feel is not true. **Do not deceive yourself.** Your wariness may not occur on the first date. It may be a little later, but you know deep down inside that something is not right.

The truth always shows itself. Give it some time, and a person's true character will come forward. A person's true motives will present themselves. Who he really is, his issues will come to the forefront. Is he kind and loving, or is he mean-spirited and abusive? Does he love you for you, or is he with you for what you can do for him? Is he a man you want to be with, or should you move on? The truth always has a way of revealing itself. You must be willing to accept the truth when it does.

Talk is cheap. Words are cheap. Actions speak louder than words. The truth is shown not only by what is said, but also by what is done. Just as a person's actions can dictate who they are, actions can reveal how he values you. Do not always assume the worse or distrust everything that is said, but do not be gullible. That is, weigh his words by his actions.

Trust your gut. Usually, a person puts his or her best foot forward in the beginning of a relationship, anyway. So, it truly takes spending time with someone, in person or via phone, for the truth to reveal itself. Yet, if at any time there is an indication that something is not right – SOMETHING IS NOT RIGHT. **Your Gut Never Lies.** He is not the man for you.

Use your God-given common sense. Do not ignore that warning. Do not ignore that inner voice. Some people say it's a woman's intuition, a sixth sense, the Holy Spirit; no matter how small it seems, no matter how quiet the voice, it is still a warning. When you do not heed or you ignore the warning, when you go against your instincts, YOU ARE THE PERSON WHO WILL SUFFER. You are the person who ultimately pays a price.

All that glitters, ain't gold. There are no perfect men. No man is a golden god. Everyone has shortcomings; everyone has issues. He may appear to be the perfect man, but appearances can be deceiving. If you get the inkling that he is not being truthful, that he is hiding something, that there is more to this man than what he presents, then know, there is more to this man than what he presents. Do not ignore the feeling; do not ignore the warning. It is in your best interest to know the truth about the man you are dating. So, if it is <u>too good</u> to be true, it is too good to <u>be true.</u>

Ignorance is NOT bliss. Do not ignore the truth. Do not turn a blind eye and then act surprised when the truth presents or reveals itself; do not be surprised when you go against your instincts, and the matter comes back to bite you later. Neither avoidance nor denial will make a problem that you see go away or issues that are evident disappear. It is better to know about something unpleasant, than to not know. At the very least, you can make an informed decision, a decision based on all of the facts. Even if it is the wrong decision, you are not entering into the relationship blindly and clueless.

There are no open books. Even though he says his life is an open book, the book is only "open" to the pages that he wants you to read. He will only show you those pages that he wants you to see. He will not show you the skeletons in his closet. He does not want you to know about certain chapters of his life. ("Oh no, don't look back there.") He may act like an open book, but in reality, you are only reading the pages he is showing you.

Seeing is believing. When a man shows you that he is mean-spirited, or tells you about his character, listen to him. When he makes statements like, "I will not allow a woman to do that," or "If a woman does this to me I will...," then BELIEVE IT! He is speaking the truth. He knows himself better than you do. We think, he will love me enough that he will not act that way, or he wouldn't do that to me. Do not be a fool. Do not deceive yourself. If it looks like a duck, and sounds like a duck, it is a duck!

When in doubt, don't do it. If you are feeling wary, cautious, hesitant, unsure, reluctant, uncomfortable, ill at ease; if your spirit is restless, if your skin starts to crawl or itch, if you do not have peace, or you are fearful in any way, **DON'T DO IT**. Do not date this man. Do not date him again! End the relationship! **YOUR SAFETY IS YOUR FIRST PRIORITY!!**

Learn from your mistakes. You are going to do stupid things and make foolish decisions in life. You will probably date the wrong man. You will more than likely suffer a broken heart. However, it is important that you learn from your mistakes, and not forget the route you took to get there, to make sure that you do not repeat the same mistakes. You have probably heard the expression, "when you forget your past, you are bound to repeat it." **Do not repeat the same cycle of failure**.

He Loves You, Not

Chapter 5: Hear Those Around You

Many times, we hear what people say, but we do not listen. Because most of us are single-minded when it comes to our relationships, we fail to see the full picture; we fail to be objective. As a result, we feel blind-sided when the relationship is not successful, when the relationship comes to the end. We are sometimes dumbfounded by the fact that we failed to see the end coming.

There are those in the crowd, some closest to us, who try to give advice, or shout out a warning. However, when it comes to the one we are attracted to, we do not or will not even <u>hear</u> what others have to say. Simply put, we <u>reject</u> what is being said to us.

A classmate wrote in my 6th grade Autograph Book,

>Don't make love by the garden gate, 'cause love is blind,
>but the neighbors ain't.

The truth of the matter is that those around you have a perspective you do not have. They are not "blinded." It is true that bias, or jealousy may prompt them to speak unkindly, but they possess an objectivity you lack. Because they are outsiders looking in, they definitely can see things about your relationship or about the man you are dating.

You may choose to ignore a comment made by your mother, your sister, your best friend, or your girlfriends. Nonetheless, when you decide to <u>hear</u> those around you, you may find that there is consistency and truth in what they say.

They especially, give you an indication when something is <u>not</u> right. It could be what is not said, i.e. reactions from co-workers or friends, to that individual. It could be a negative comment, or two, about your relationship or that person. On the other hand, they may state it as blatant and direct as "He is not good enough for you. He is not right for you. I don't trust him."

Additionally, when different people are telling you the same message, or giving you the same advice and they do not know or speak with one another, then you have to realize that the advice is a confirmation of the truth. Nevertheless, no matter how it is "said", you can choose to ignore it, or you can choose to <u>hear</u>.

Hearing does not mean listening. When you listen you are processing thoughts, you are processing what is being said. Hearing is your ears acting as a messenger – your ears are just bringing the information to your brain. So because you hear what a person is saying, does not mean you are processing the message.

Sometimes people give you bad advice, advice they themselves would not follow, or advice you are just not interested in following. So you may decide not to listen to the advice given by friends or family, but do not be afraid to <u>hear</u> what is being said. Do not automatically reject what you hear, because you do not like the message.

Eat the meat and discard the bones. Again, people tend to give you advice that they themselves will not follow. For that reason, not all advice given will <u>apply</u> to you, but some things <u>may</u> be helpful to you. Therefore, do not discount everything that is said. Either it is for you, or it is not for you. Regardless of how it is said, if it does not apply to you, let it go. Take what you need, what you can use, and discard the rest.

Recognize the truth when you hear it. It is often difficult to hear the truth, especially, when in your heart, you <u>know</u> it to be the truth. You tend to first deny it, and then reject what is being said to you. The truth sometimes stings, and can oftentimes be very painful to hear. However, when you recognize the truth, you accept the validity of the thing being said to you or at the very least, you should acknowledge and not ignore that it is being said. When you recognize the truth, you are in a better position to consider or think on the matter, in order to make smarter decisions.

Seek Godly Counsel. There is some advice that you will never follow. There are those in the crowd who do not wish you well, who are naysayers – that is, they are contrary and negative because of their own issues, and will therefore, give you unsound advice. When there are too many voices, and you are not sure whose advice to follow, seek counsel from someone you trust, someone whom you know knows the Lord. Whether they are a Pastor, a Christian counselor, a co-worker or relative whom you know professes Jesus Christ as their Lord and Savior, they will give you wise, Godly counsel.

There are many Scriptures that address the benefit of Godly counsel:

> Without counsel, plans go awry, but in the multitude of

counselors they are established.
(Proverbs 15:22, NKJV)

Hear counsel, and receive instruction, that thou mayest be wise in thy latter end.
(Proverbs 19:20, KJV)

There are many devices in a man's heart; nevertheless the counsel of the LORD, that shall stand.
(Proverbs 19:21, KJV)

Blessed is the man that walketh not in the counsel of the ungodly, nor standeth in the way of sinners, nor sitteth in the seat of the scornful.
(Psalm 1:1, KJV)

The way of a fool is right in his own eyes: but he that hearkeneth unto counsel is wise.
(Proverbs 12:15, KJV)

So do not be a fool. Be willing to receive wise, Godly counsel from others.

Hindsight is 20/20. You always have 20/20 vision when you are looking back. With the benefit of hindsight, you are able to judge your experiences with a different perspective. Situations are clearer; you are able to pinpoint almost with complete accuracy where you went wrong, or where a problem or discrepancy first arose in the relationship. However, in most cases, after the fact is too late.

When you choose to hear, not only will others give you an indication that you are being used or mistreated, that something is just not right, but conversely, they cause you to take stock of your own actions, to evaluate where you are at fault, or are mistreating your mate. Those around you may say, "He is a good man, do not mess up." "It's not worth it, leave it alone." "You need to treat him better or you will lose him." Get a clue! Remember, those around you definitely see things you may not, and by choosing to hear, you may be able to make the correction, or to rectify the situation while you still have time.

Often you do not know what you have until you lose it, anyway. You realize in retrospect what you had once it is gone; you recognize how valuable it was to you when it is no longer yours. By hearing those around you, at the very least you are forewarned, then you can choose to heed their warning(s) or not.

Others are so often right. My experience has been that your family and friends will see things that you are too blind to see, especially, the older adults. They possess experience and wisdom that you sometimes lack. They have been down the road you currently are on, and can warn you against traveling it.

It does not matter that you are grown. If they have traveled a road and can say to you "don't go down that road, because there is a big gaping hole, there are hoops of fire to jump through and a cliff at the end," would you not want to know it? Moreover, how many times have you said, "I wish I knew then, what I know now"?

Unfortunately, for me there was some advice that I did not heed until it was too late. Nevertheless, I found that when I chose to hear what was being said, I was able to incorporate what I learned into my next relationship.

Do not be Young and Dumb or Old and Stupid. Aahh, youth. Sometimes when we are young, we do the dumbest things. This is usually due to ignorance, a lack of knowledge, or a lack of experience. Hopefully, we learn from those experiences, and make better decisions.

However, there are some who still make <u>stupid</u> choices as they age. You many times attribute these choices to stubbornness, being set in your ways, unwillingness to change, or refusing to listen. Remember, <u>whatever</u> decisions you make, whatever choices you elect, YOU WILL HAVE TO LIVE WITH THEM! So learn from those experiences, and make better choices.

Feel free to revisit what others have said. Certain advice may not fit your current circumstance, but it may apply to a different circumstance, at a later date. Although you could not receive what others were saying then, for some reason, you can hear them now. Retrieve the advice from your mental folder, and feel free to apply it to your current situation; it is still good advice, and will probably save you some heartache and definitely, some headache.

So hear those around you. It will make you smarter, and you will do some things differently, the next time.

He Loves You, Not

Chapter 6: Sex before Marriage

Growing up, I wish that I was told, "Don't have sex until you are married," and "It's okay to not be sexually active." In my household, my parents would talk to me about birth control, protecting myself when I have sex. My father and mother were teenagers when I was born; hence, I was unplanned. I am sure they believed that they were protecting me from making a similar mistake when they placed me on birth control pills at the age 15. I was not sexually active at the time; I was still a virgin. In fact, it was because I was on the pill that I felt it was alright to have sex, because I knew that I would not get pregnant.

My early sexual activity eventually led to promiscuous behavior, because sex was something I really enjoyed. My promiscuity rarely led to a meaningful relationship. I tried to rationalize my behavior by using terms like sexships, or friends with "benefits." This simply meant that we were friends, but I was giving all of the physical benefits of a relationship without receiving any emotional attachment. I quickly discovered that the "benefit" was not mine, because no matter how hard I tried to justify the lack of a committed relationship in my life, I still sought it; I still longed for it. Had I waited to have sex, at the very least, I could have avoided a lot of heartache. Like myself, so many women do not wait to have sex, and many are very promiscuous.

Unmarried Sex

Becoming sexually active at an early age forces you to grow up very quickly, and act more mature than you really are. As a teen and young adult, you are still developing emotionally, physically and psychologically. With early sex, you make an emotional and psychological investment, when in fact, you do not know <u>yourself</u>. At this age, you are still figuring out who you are, your own likes and dislikes, and where you fit in. Moreover, it is a time where you are combating peer pressure, esteem issues, body and personal image. Intimacy adds a dynamic and pressure for which most young people are not ready.

Because premarital sex is not love, it can only lead to pain and disappointment when you are seeking that love. The Bible says that when two people are married, they become one flesh. "For this cause shall a man leave his father and mother, and shall be joined unto his wife, and they two shall be one flesh." (Ephesians 5:31, KJV) Sex is the consummation of the marital union. Therefore, when two people break off their relationship after having sex, it is like ripping apart flesh. This rip in the relationship often causes an internal/emotional struggle, which is more difficult to manage when you are a teen and young adult. This also explains why engaging in premarital sex causes you to become so dependent upon the person to whom you give your body.

Becoming sexually active at an early age also creates adult problems. These are problems that can be avoided by waiting. For example, sexually transmitted diseases (STDs), AIDS, unwanted pregnancy, abortion, infertility, children out of wedlock, anger, bitterness, or hardness of heart.

Additionally, when you engage in premarital sex, you open yourself up to people and experiences that you really should not be exposed to – indiscriminate sex, sex with multiple partners, promiscuity, lewdness, same-sex partners, one-night stands, or illicit sex. You may obtain a reputation of being a freak, a slut, or a whore, or you may exchange sex or sexual favors for money or material things, then are bound by feelings of guilt, shame and regret, as a result of your behavior.

Engaging in varying and multiple sex acts causes your appetite/lust to become greater. It takes more and more to satisfy you. Normal sexual intimacy is no longer enough. It no longer fulfills you. You seek over the top exploits, and acrobatics for fulfillment. Consequently, when you finally marry, you risk bringing the negative aspects of these experiences into your marriage; it is as if you are inviting these people and these aberrant experiences into your bedroom.

Additionally, the lust may cause you to think about these other individuals, these previous experiences, while you are with your mate. You may have memories of more skilled partners with whom you are constantly comparing your spouse. You then expect your spouse to match or exceed that skill level, to fulfill the lust, to feed the monster you have created, the lust you have mentally indulged. And when he is unable to, because he may not have these lust issues, or he may not go along with these sex acts, sex becomes a stumbling block, causing your relationship to suffer.

Married Sex

Sex is a beautiful God-given activity that is wonderful when practiced within the boundaries of a marriage. Sex is the completion of the binding of two people within marriage; it is a God-given gift.

Waiting until marriage to have sex gives you freedom from guilt, shame, lust and regret. Ideally, you are in a committed relationship with someone you love, honor, respect and trust. You can share an intimacy that is special and meaningful.

There is also an oneness that occurs. You are receiving a part of him and he is receiving a part of you. Have you ever noticed how married couples start to act, talk, and think alike? They even look alike. This is because they are truly one.

> Therefore shall a man leave his father and his mother, and shall cleave unto his wife: and they shall be one flesh.
> (Genesis 2:24, KJV)

Additionally, God honors sex in marriage.

> Marriage is honourable in all, and the bed undefiled: but whoremongers and adulterers God will judge. (Hebrews 13:4, KJV)

As I have stated previously, I wish I was told, "Don't have sex until you are married, that it's okay to <u>not</u> be sexually active." My parents were not saved individuals. They did not know Jesus Christ as their personal Savior; therefore, they did not teach me how to live by the Word of God.

The Bible clearly teaches what God expects of unmarried men and women, that you should not fornicate – that is, have sex when you are not married. That you should:

> Flee fornication. Every sin that a man doeth is without the body; but he that committeth fornication sinneth against his own body.
>
> What? know ye not that your body is the temple of the Holy Ghost which is in you,

> which ye have of God, and ye are not your own?
>
> For ye are bought with a price: therefore glorify God in your body, and in your spirit, which are God's.
> (I Corinthians 6:18-20, KJV)

Moreover, the Bible teaches why it is important that you wait until you are married:

> For this is the will of God, even your sanctification, that ye should abstain from fornication: That every one of you should know how to possess his vessel in sanctification and honour.
>
> For God hath not called us unto uncleanness, but to holiness.
> (I Thessalonians 4:3-4, and 7, KJV)
>
> Nevertheless, to avoid

> fornication, let every man have his own wife, and let every woman have her own husband.
> (I Corinthians 7:2, KJV)

If you wait, as the Scriptures say, you only know your husband, and therefore, avoid carrying baggage into your marriage.

Additionally, there is a benefit in waiting. When we wait on God and we are obedient to His Word by not engaging in premarital sex, God honors our obedience. Waiting, that is, being obedient produces the blessings from God.

> The Lord is good unto them that wait for Him, to the soul that seeketh him. It is good that a man should both hope and quietly wait for the salvation of the Lord.
> (Lamentations 3:25-26, KJV)

> And therefore will the LORD wait, that he may be gracious unto you, and therefore will he be exalted, that he may have mercy upon

you: for the LORD is a God of judgment: blessed are all they that wait for him. (Isaiah 30:18, KJV)

Therefore, to you Ladies who have never heard it from anyone else:

It is okay to <u>not</u> be sexually active, and DO NOT have sex until you are married.

He Loves You, Not

Chapter 7: If It Is Not Working, Know When to Call It Quits

There comes a point in the relationship that <u>you know</u> it is over. It may be on the first date. Did he ask you for your number, or ask you out again? It could be subtle in that you see things are winding to a close; you do not talk as much, and/or go out as much. His behavior has changed; you are no longer that special someone. You sense he is seeing another person or persons; he is avoiding you. It could be as blatant as a phone call or direct conversation where he tells you it is over.

There is a point in the relationship, when you know it is over. It may be expected or unexpected. It may really hurt, or you yourself may be ready to move on. But KNOW WHEN TO CALL IT QUITS.

Holding on to relationships is very unhealthy. Besides the hurt and pain, it causes your behavior to become very irrational. You act crazy. You manifest signs of jealousy, and possessiveness. You create havoc in his life. The man receives unwarranted treatment, because you are not ready to end it.

Why do you hold on?

- <u>You hold on because of religious beliefs, tradition, or custom</u>. Because your mother remained with your father all those years unwavering in her vows in spite of his mess, or because your Aunt Bessie stayed in an abusive relationship, you believe that you are obligated to "stick with your man", regardless of the circumstances.

  Whereas, your mother was taught that divorce is taboo, and more significantly, because her religious beliefs, her values, and customs have been instilled in you, you too remain in a dysfunctional relationship. However, no one should be subject to an abusive relationship, whether it is verbal, physical, mental or emotional.

  Additionally, you know in your heart of hearts, (and your mother can probably tell you herself) that she should have left him. Nevertheless, she stayed, because she was expected to, because divorce was frowned upon, and because things were different in her generation, (<u>her</u> parents never divorced). However, if you are at that point that you <u>know</u> the relationship is truly over, <u>let</u> <u>it</u> <u>go</u>!

- <u>You hold on because of fear</u>. You fear being lonely or alone. You fear that you will never meet any one like him, or as good as him. You may fear being seen as a failure by your friends or family. You may be embarrassed, because your friends and family love him and think he is the best thing since sliced bread. You may be embarrassed by the prospect of a break up, especially, when everyone else around you is a couple, appears to be happy together, or their relationship seems to be working out.

    Do not be deceived, because you know that things are not always, what they seem. You really do not know for sure if what these couples are portraying is the truth.

Additionally, if you do not let go, you will never find out if there is another man as good as or better than he is, because you are not in a position to meet him.

Furthermore, no one can walk in your shoes; your friends and family members do not <u>truly</u> know what is occurring in your relationship. **Do not allow your mother and father, your girlfriends to talk you into holding onto a relationship that you do not want, that <u>you</u> <u>know</u> is not for you.** YOU HAVE TO DO WHAT IS BEST FOR YOU!

- <u>You hold on because you are vulnerable, because your self-esteem has taken a beaten</u>. In Chapter 10, we talk about how low self-esteem causes you to compromise. You feel unworthy, ugly, unlovable and start to doubt yourself. You take the blame and begin to accept unhealthy behavior, dysfunctional behavior. For example, you accept the fact that your mate is unfaithful. You feel that as long as he comes home to you, sleeps in your bed, pays the bills, or takes care of home, you can look the other way.

Eventually those indiscretions, those "outside" situations will come home to you and you will have to face the repercussions of the other relationships. No matter how long you have allowed the situation to continue or how many years you have overlooked his unfaithful behavior, eventually, those "issues" will come to you. JUST BECAUSE YOU LOOK THE OTHER WAY, DOES NOT MAKE A PROBLEM GO AWAY.

- <u>You hold on because you form emotional attachments</u>. Because it is easier to hold on than to let go, because you fear change, do not like change, or do not want to change. Because you still love him, or you think you are still in love.

  Love is a very powerful emotion, but love is sometimes DOING WHAT

YOU KNOW IS BEST FOR HIM. If that means letting him go, let him go.

- <u>You hold on because although you may not want him, you do not want anyone else to have him</u>. These thoughts are representative of unstable, jealous, possessive, and stalker-like behavior. Check yourself!

- <u>You hold on because you have put the time into the relationship</u>. You have a history with him; you may have children, or you have invested a good portion of your life and feel that he "owes" you. You believed that you could change him, but a leopard cannot change his spots, nor a zebra erase his stripes. He is who he is, and holding on will not change him.

- <u>You hold on because you are blinded by good sex</u>. Let's face it the sex is good. Period! It is the difference between a good cup of coffee and a bad cup. The bad cup you never want again; the good cup you want over and over, so you hold on. The problem is that when you are not having sex, the relationship lacks substance, the relationship is in disarray, and you are unhappy. IT TAKES MORE THAN SEX TO SUSTAIN A LASTING RELATIONSHIP. So if you are holding on just for the sex, the lack of substance will ultimately leave you feeling unfulfilled.

It is important that you are cognizant of your conduct, and that you monitor your reaction and your behavior when your relationship is over.

Quit being Jealous. You become bitter, resentful, and envious. It causes you to be another person, a person you yourself dislike. Jealousy causes you to behave in a way that will later cause you shame.

Jealousy makes you ugly. It does not matter how beautiful your outward appearance may be. When jealousy, anger, envy or bitterness manifests itself through you, when these flaws or defects in your character arise, you appear to be ugly.

Do not Lash Out. Do not be mean, angry, nasty, petty, spiteful or vindictive toward him. Do not try to hurt him, or destroy his property. Let it go…

Do not Cling. Let him go. Return his belongings. Stop calling him, texting him, emailing him, etc. Stop leaving him messages, or calling and hanging up. He is not stupid; he knows it is you. He will <u>never</u> want to deal with you again. If he sees you, HE WILL AVOID YOU.

Don't be a Hater. Do not hate on him, do not wish him harm, do not wish the worst for him, do not resent the fact that he has moved on. Do not waste your time and energy hating him. You must move on; you must let him go.

Do not Manipulate him with Sex. Sex is only a temporary measure. It will not repair the relationship, or solve the problems that caused your relationship to end.

Do not use the kids against him. Your children did not ask to be here, nor do they need to be involved in the details of your relationship. You do not have to talk down about him, put him down or tear him down in the eyes of your children. Kids are smart, and will figure things out for themselves pretty quickly. When you use your children as pawns in your relationship, it can affect their self-esteem. It can make them feel a lack of security, and cause them to worry. It can also affect their future relationships with men and women, causing them to be resentful, spiteful, and distrusting.

Using your children as pawns also teaches them that it is acceptable to use and/or manipulate others. They learn to become calculating and undermining, they lose their character, and they lack the integrity they should have – they use whatever it takes to get ahead. They become that person that you cannot trust, that person whom you always wonder about their true motives, because <u>you</u> taught them that it is alright to use people for their own self interest and personal gain. You have taught them that it is alright to walk on people and treat them like dirt. Remember, children learn from observation, association, and their environment; they learn from cause and effect. Children will do what you teach them; the apple will not fall far from the tree.

Keep your Integrity. Integrity is honesty; it is being upright. It is doing what you know is right regardless of the circumstance, how you feel, how hurt or angry you are. Do not compromise who you are, keep your dignity and your self-respect. Do not behave in a way that you will later regret.

Cut your Losses. Do not invest more into the relationship when you know the relationship is over. That is, do not believe you will get a return on your investment when all factors point to the contrary. He will not change; he will not be the man you were hoping he would be. Cut your losses and move on.

It is what it is. Face the facts – it's over. Some things cannot be changed. Even when we change our behavior temporarily, or if we compromise, we step out of character, or act in a way that is unbecoming, the facts have not changed – it is not working out. Pull yourself together, and move on.

Avoid the emotional rollercoaster. The breaking up, getting back together, to break up again cycle takes a toll on your emotions. It affects your mental or physical health, in that, it causes you to be anxious and focused solely on your relationship. You may lose or gain weight, become depressed, anti-social or reclusive. This is at the cost of other significant areas in your life, like paying your bills, and dealing with your responsibilities. Additionally, the effect of the emotional rollercoaster is that you end up repeating the same sense of grief and loss in the final break-up as you did in the initial break-up.

Do not become the girlfriend or date whom he remembers as being the lunatic. Stop calling constantly, leaving nasty messages, calling other women in his cell phone phonebook, or slandering his name. Do not follow him or stalk him, show up at his job, his home, or where he hangs out with his "boys." Stop trying to solicit information about him from his friends and family. They are on his side, not yours.

A break-up does not have to equal drama. You can end your relationship with mutual respect. Yes, you may be hurt, but you do not have to take cheap shots, or say mean and hurtful words, because you want to get back at him. When the situation warrants it, be the bigger person. You can be truthful, and express how you feel, without the drama.

Do not burn every bridge. Not all relationships warrant an abrupt ending, or a complete and utter termination. In some situations, you and he may be able to remain friends, once you are past the hurt and anger. He is a person who knows you, and will give you sincere, honest and straightforward advice in your future relationships.

You reap what you sow. If you sow havoc and discord, you reap havoc and discord. If you sow envy and jealousy, you reap envy and jealousy. There are repercussions to your actions. Everything you do comes back to you. "Be not deceived; God is not mocked: for whatsoever a man soweth, that shall he also reap." (Galatians 6:7, KJV) Therefore, take care of how you treat others, because that same treatment will be repaid to you in your lifetime. What you do now comes back upon you later.

Chapter 8: Do Not Force It, Get Off the Ride

Relationships have stages; they have a natural progression. (See Relationship Flow Chart, p. 105)

Upon meeting, there has to be a mutual attraction. There is something that you like about him that makes you interested in getting to know him. It could be his looks, his sense of style, or his sense of humor. You perceive that he is someone worth getting to know.

- ♦ When there is no attraction, or no interest, **do not force it.** You get off the ride, and you do not move on to the dating stage.

Date

When dating, there must be chemistry, or some sort of connection (not sexual). Dating gives you the opportunity to get to know him. Is he giving or selfish? Does he fall into the category of a man who causes alarm, a man who produces flashing red lights, bells and whistles, or is he a person you would like to continue seeing and getting to know?

Dating allows you to ascertain what <u>you</u> like and dislike in a man, and what you will tolerate. Dating broadens your options; you do not need to settle for less than you deserve in a relationship.

- ♦ When there is no chemistry, a lack of interest, or you see personality traits that you dislike, get off the ride. **Do not force it**; staying with a man you are not attracted to, is settling. Do not date him again. Move on and date someone else. However, if you find that you are compatible, develop a friendship with him.

Friendship

Friendship promotes mutual respect and more significantly, trust. You are comfortable with one another. You enjoy each other's company. You can be honest with one another. You get to know the real person. Friendship allows you to learn about who he is, his personality, his flaws, his issues, his interests, his childhood, his family life, his goals, and his dreams.

- ♦ Developing friendships are invaluable, in that if you have to get off the ride, you can at the very least remain friends, and true friends are often hard to come by.

Commitment

If your goal is to be in a committed relationship, with the prospect of marriage, then it is only natural that you are willing to put the time and energy into the relationship by dating and becoming friends. You merit sufficient loyalty, trust, respect and chemistry that you <u>want</u> to put some quality time into the relationship.

At this stage, you should be in love. You should have intense feelings of tender affection and compassion, along with strong passionate romantic desire. It is a stage where the birds sing, the flowers are in bloom, your heart sings, you have stars in your eyes; you are in love.

♪♪ LOVE, LOVE, LOVE ♪♪

This is a point in your relationship where you should be exclusive – you know enough about him that you <u>want</u> to be with him. You understand you love one another; you are boyfriend and girlfriend. Your friends, family, co-workers, <u>know</u> that you are together, and are in a committed relationship.

- If the relationship deteriorates, and you have to get off the ride, you may remain friends, or you go your separate ways, but **do not force**

Do Not Force it,
Get Off the Ride

it. If it is not working out, let him go. You know when it is truly over, when you have tried to make it work, but it is not working. Most times the emotional connection or bond is broken, before the physical separation ever occurs.

Marriage

Your goal is to get to the altar, and spend your life with him. You have put the time in, you know enough about him that you want to build a life with him, raise a family, and grow old with him. Marriage is the stage where you will truly discover who he is.

Some things you will not learn about him, or see about him until you live with him day in and day out. Sometimes there are latent expectations of what he wants from a wife in marriage, which are a different standard than what he wanted from a girlfriend.

- ♦ It should not be so easy to get off this ride. The stakes are a lot higher, so you do not want to give up so easily. Getting off the ride at this stage leads to separation and divorce.

Healing

Experience dictates that ending a relationship will affect you in some way, regardless of which stage you are in when you get off the ride. Should you feel any hurt, grief, emotional distress, or anguish once the relationship is over, then you need time to heal.

Healing is a process. No one can define for you the time it takes to heal from the pain of a newly ended relationship. Chapter 9 discusses overcoming a broken heart. How it takes time for a broken heart to mend, how you _can_ and _will_ survive the break-up. Taking the time needed to heal will give you the opportunity to find closure, to attain peace with your newly found circumstances. Healing is an important step in your journey, for it is necessary to be healthy and whole as you move forward, and start anew.

Do Not Force it,
Get Off the Ride

Relationship Flow Chart

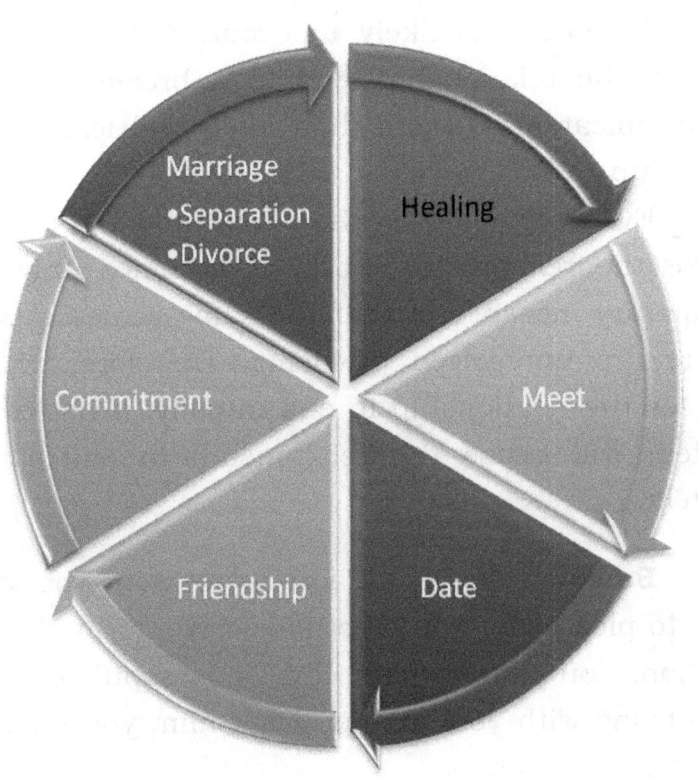

Forcing a relationship is counter-productive. You cannot jump from one stage of the relationship to another without experiencing trauma or drama; you miss some key developments, consequently. Although you may attempt to recover or recapture these missed stages, serious strain to the relationship is likely to occur. Not only will forcing the relationship lead to a breakdown in communication, it more than likely will lead to a break-up.

Even when you reach a truce, and you try to make the relationship work, it becomes only a temporary measure in that the same issues exist. There are unresolved problems. Therefore, what causes the relationship to end initially, if not corrected, will cause the relationship to end ultimately.

Be yourself. Do not act like someone you are not, to please him, or keep him. It is a form of deception. You cannot make him or manipulate him into being with you. By deceiving him, you create two major dilemmas:

> 1) You become a liar. You are not being honest with him or yourself. Not only is this a farce that you will have to perpetuate as

long as you are in a relationship with him, it is also unhealthy for your mental health and well-being.

Additionally, if he is not accepting of the <u>real</u> you early on in the relationship, he definitely will not receive a complete change in your personality later. That is, when you finally decide to be yourself, he will not know who you are, but more damagingly, he will not trust that you are the person you say you are.

2) Failure to be you also creates dual or multiple personalities. Who are you really? Are you Dr. Jekyll or Mr. Hyde?[3] You are one person with your friends or co-workers, another with your family, and another with him. You keep changing to fit into the relationship, so the real you is lost, or manifests herself only on occasion.

Additionally, do not be so consumed with being what others need you to be, or what they want you to be, that you are no longer yourself. Being someone other than who you <u>are</u>, or constantly trying to please others, wears you down mentally, takes its toll on you emotionally, and becomes a burden to your happiness. You can only be you – be the best you that you can be. Be yourself; you will be healthier and happier in the long-run.

Do not enter a relationship unless you know and like who <u>you</u> are. A relationship cannot meet your deepest (self) love need. No <u>man</u> can meet your deepest love need. Your man is not your father, so if you are looking for daddy, do not get involved. Your man will not validate you, that is to make you feel valued as a person; so if you are with him because you need to feel worthy or build your esteem, do not get involved. **Only Christ can meet your deepest love need.**

> In this was manifested the love of God toward us, because that God sent his only begotten Son in to the world, that we might live through him. Herein is love, not that we loved God, but that he loved us, and sent his Son to

be the propitiation[1] for our sins.
(I John 4:9-10, KJV)

[Moreover,] we love him, because he first loved us.
(I John 4:19, KJV)

A RELATIONSHIP DOES NOT MAKE YOU WHO YOU ARE; A RELATIONSHIP WILL NOT MAKE YOU WHOLE. You must come to the relationship WHOLE. You must be comfortable with whom you are, you must know who you are. Only Christ can make you whole: "As ye have therefore received Christ Jesus the Lord, so walk ye in him...For in him dwelleth all the fullness of the Godhead bodily. And ye are complete in him, which is the head of all principality and power." (Colossians 2:6, 9-10, KJV) You must love yourself, if you hope to be a suitable mate to someone else. Unless you know and like who you are...STAY SINGLE.

Meet people where they are. Meet him where he is. Do not try to change him. Do not

---

[1] *Atoning sacrifice*

think that you can change him. Meet him where he is and if he is not the man for you, leave him there.

I repeat, **MEET PEOPLE WHERE THEY ARE.** Do not think that you can change him. If he is not the man for you, leave him where he is.

Been there, done that. You know when you have been down a road before. If you see the same pattern occurring, or the same progression in a relationship and you know it did not work before, get off the ride. A fool can be defined as a person who does the same thing repeatedly, expecting a different outcome. Why subject yourself to the same frustration, or the same disappointment? "As a dog returns to its vomit, so a fool repeats his folly." (Proverbs 26.11, NIV) Do not be a fool, close that chapter, and get off the ride.

Do not read more into the relationship than what there really is. You cannot force a square peg into a round hole. You cannot make a person like you or force a person to love you, to have a relationship with you, or even to do right within the relationship. He has to make a choice. It has to come from him; he has to decide if this is a relationship worth pursuing, worth investing in.

Do Not Force it,
Get Off the Ride

Even if you try to make it work by doing all the things that you are suppose to do, or you believe you are suppose to do, simply put, it really is what it is. If the feeling is not mutual, then get off the ride. No matter how hard you try, you cannot make someone want you, call you, pursue you, want to call you, and want to be with you or spend time with you. If his response is not from the heart and truly genuine, then his "feelings" will not last for the duration of the relationship. "For where your treasure is, there will your heart be also." (Matthew 6:21, KJV) So if he does not treasure you, you do not have his heart. Conversely, if his heart is not into you, then he will not treasure you.

Do not allow him to string you along. In some situations, a man will not break up with a woman until he has solidified another relationship. In chapter 7, we addressed how we know when a relationship is over and how we hold on to relationships even when it is not working out. Therefore, if you get the inkling or even suspect that he is holding on to you while seeing someone else, immediately GET OFF THE RIDE!

You know what you know. You usually know when the relationship is changing, or has changed. There is a feeling that somehow manifests itself. Even if you try to deny it, you know what you know. The last person you want to deceive is yourself.

Accept the facts. Unless you both are willing to resolve the issues in the relationship, the ride is more than likely coming to an end. One party alone cannot make the relationship work. Do not deceive yourself; get off the ride.

Do not be afraid to get off the ride. Do not be afraid to leave him or to lose him. Fear causes you to be bound and to not make any move at all. You may be afraid of being alone. You fear you will never meet someone like him. You fear never marrying, or ever having children. If the relationship is not working out, get off the ride. Do not be afraid to move on.

Do not compromise and accept a relationship where you are unhappy. Do not settle and accept behavior that is unhealthy for you. If it is not the right fit, doesn't feel right, or if you are consistently unhappy, move on. You will date again. There will be someone else, and <u>he</u> may be

Do Not Force it,
Get Off the Ride

the person for you. However, if you do not get off the ride, you will never know...

He Loves You, Not

Chapter 9: Overcoming a Broken Heart

To overcome is to struggle successfully against a difficulty or disadvantage and to conquer it.[4]

We have all experienced a broken heart. The hurt, loss, pain, grief, disappointment, sadness, distress, anguish, and even despair, associated with relationship woes. However, you can overcome a broken heart, especially, in spite of the obstacles – the pain, the grief, and the hurt.

There are many causes for a broken heart: disappointment, broken promises, broken vows, rejection, affairs, adultery, betrayal of trust, lack of chemistry, loss of attraction, lack of commitment, abusive or unhealthy relationships, you are not in love with him or you love him more than he loves you, failure to trust your gut, or failure to follow your heart. Whatever the cause may be, being broken-hearted is a very painful experience.

A broken heart can make you angry and bitter. A broken heart can make you feel incapacitated, vulnerable, helpless, and out of control. It may cause you to feel depressed and hopeless about the prospect of finding future love.

Part of the problem is that you dwell on the relationship. That is, in your mind you relive the moments you have had with him. Either you focus solely on the good times ignoring the bad, or conversely, you become fixated on your <u>great</u> loss, and subject yourself to a pity party. Either way you are stuck and unable to move past this place. Because you continually relive those moments, you begin to miss him more and more, hence, you long for what was.

However, you <u>can</u> survive a broken heart. You can come through this experience and period of difficulty, and continue to function. Unfortunately, you may have some (emotional) bumps and bruises, as a result, but you <u>will</u> live through this.

IT TAKES TIME. It takes time to forget. It will take time for the pain to diminish, and eventually, to go away. It takes time for your heart to mend. A broken heart is like an open wound – it needs time to heal properly. You have to <u>go</u> through, <u>grow</u> through, and <u>then</u> you heal.

Take it one day at a time. Healing is a process. There is no quick fix, no formula, no magic potion, and no set period for a broken heart to mend. Some broken hearts mend more quickly than others do. What is important is that you give yourself the time <u>you</u> need to heal. Since the situation cannot get any worse, it will only get better. Be fair to yourself, and give yourself time.

Accept the truth. The truth is that you are no longer with him. The truth is that you heart <u>is</u> broken. You <u>are</u> in pain. And you need time to heal.

Face the grief and the loss. Do not avoid grieving. Do not deny the pain. If you shield yourself from the grief, then it will always be with you. Once you grieve, you can begin to heal and move past the hurt. You need to take it in, go through it and deal with the loss.

Allow the Lord to heal you. There is an expression that applies: There is no sorrow that heaven can't heal. That is, any pain, hurt, grief, distress, despair, depression, when you go to the Lord with these worries, with these burden, He can heal you. God is greater than any hurt. When you lay your burden at His feet, He can ease the pain; He can mend your broken heart; He can comfort you.

"Casting all your care upon him; for he careth for you." (I Peter 5:7, KJV)

Forget your past, but do not ignore it. Let go of the past and do not let yourself get stuck constantly wondering "what if" and "had I only..." Do not live in the past and do not let the past prevent you from moving forward.

> Forget the former things; do not dwell on the past. See, I am doing a new thing! Now it springs up; do you not perceive it? I am making a way in the desert and streams in the wasteland. (Isaiah 43.18-19, NIV)

Focusing on yesterday can cause you to hang on to the pain, tragedy or regret of yesterday. Learn from your mistakes, setbacks, and lack of success and move on.

Relationships come and go. Relationships fail. People fail you. You may lose friends, your mate may leave you, or your husband may walk out on you. With man, there are no guarantees.

However, even though you may feel alone or abandoned, the Lord will not desert you. "...For he hath said, I will never leave thee, nor forsake thee." (Hebrews 13:5, KJV) "...and, lo, I am with you always, even unto the end of the world." (Matthew 28:20, KJV)

Do not be bitter or angry. Do not bottle up the anger. Do not hold a grudge. Anger and bitterness can cause you to be hateful and spiteful. It pushes people away from you. Anger and bitterness becomes a festering wound that will prevent you from overcoming the hurt and pain, which will prevent you from expressing love, or receiving love.

You need to Forgive.

> And when ye stand praying, forgive, if ye have ought against any: that your Father also which is in heaven may forgive you your trespasses.
>
> But if ye do not forgive, neither will your Father which is in heaven forgive your trespasses.
> (Mark 11:25-26, KJV)

Forgiveness will help you release the anger. Forgiveness will ease your process of moving on.

Fake it until you make it. Do not let him see you sweat; do not let him see you suffer. When you see him in public, especially if he is with another woman, smile and be kind, even if you are not over him. Eventually, you will realize that it does not hurt as much, and soon, it will not hurt at all – you have moved past him.

Do not let yourself go. Do not allow your personal appearance to suffer. Always look good in public. Bathe, put on clean clothes, brush your teeth, comb your hair, wear your make-up, and look your best, even though you may not feel your best.

Do not shut down! Do not become immobilized or paralyzed. Do not stop functioning. CLEAN YOUR HOUSE. Get rid of the boxes, the trash, the extra junk you have accumulated during the relationship. Do not hold onto the clutter. The clutter is an outward manifestation of your inward condition. It represents the baggage you still have from your former relationship.

Do not self-deprecate, that is, do not put yourself down, do not belittle yourself, do not devalue your self-worth. YOU ARE NOT PERFECT. Yes, you may have played a role in the reason why the relationship ended. However, **YOU ARE NOT A FAILURE, the relationship failed**. Sometimes, no matter how hard we try to make it work, it just will not work. Consider and come to terms with the fact that the relationship was just not <u>meant</u> to be.

Restrain yourself from calling him. Do not call him. No matter how much you want to, or how badly you wish to speak to him, DO NOT CALL HIM! You want to have closure. Speaking to him will only revive the pain. It will only stir-up emotions that you are working to move past. Additionally, calling him may cause you to say something that you will later regret saying.

Stay away from break-up sex. Do not sleep with him. I repeat, DO NOT SLEEP WITH HIM! The sex may be spectacular, but is it worth the emotional setback? It is difficult enough to move past him, to move on with your life. Break-up sex recreates that emotional attachment, provides false hope, and ultimately, prolongs your healing process.

You are thinking that the sex is rekindling your relationship with him. He, on the other hand, is only in it for the sex, and not the relationship. Then when your hopes are dashed, your heart is re-broken.

Avoid Rebound Relationships. Do not be so quick to jump into another relationship. Rebound relationships are a quick fix, an emotional patch job. Rebound relationships only mask the pain. You are vulnerable. Your emotions are still unsettled, and may still be raw. YOU NEED TIME TO HEAL.

Rebound relationships will cause you to settle. Vulnerability causes you to make rash decisions, it often places you in a relationship that under normal circumstances, you would avoid. There are some men who prey on vulnerable women; who manipulate you because they know that you have experienced rejection. You later realize that this man does not truly love you, that your needs are not being met, that he was only pursuing you to fulfill his own need(s). You realize that you have been used, that you have settled.

Avoid settling. Do not accept less than you deserve. Do not compromise your standards, because of your pain. Avoid settling and you will avoid being with the wrong man.

Talk to a third party. Talk to an outsider, a person who will be objective; someone who is willing to listen, who you can vent to, and whose advice you can trust – a sister, a friend, a professional counselor or therapist. Someone who will say to you, "Do not call him. Do not have sex with him." This is a person who will talk you out of making a fool of yourself or making a foolish decision.

Do not harden your heart. Hurt causes you to build walls around your heart, to defend your heart. It can cause you to be afraid to open-up to another person. Do not let your broken heart prevent you from dating again, from loving again. You <u>are</u> worthy to receive love. You <u>are</u> capable of being loved. You <u>are</u> capable of giving love.

A broken heart is only a temporary state, and it is a normal part of life. You <u>will</u> come through this, in time. Give yourself the chance to have love in your life, again.

He Loves You, Not

Chapter 10: Learn To Love Your Self

How can you love someone else, when you do not love yourself? Failure to love yourself creates low self-esteem and a lack of self-worth. You believe you are not good enough, not pretty enough, not young enough, not thin enough, not shapely enough. Someone told you that you are not smart enough, that you are too loud, or too quiet, that your butt is too small, or your forehead is too big. You constantly compare yourself to others, because you believe you do not measure-up.

You begin to believe that if I was just like this person, or if I looked like that, I would be happy, things would be better. There is also a misguided and unsubstantiated belief that you do not deserve better. Consequently, low self-esteem, and even grief, or hurt cause many women to compromise and accept loveless relationships.

A lack of love for oneself causes you to settle. You settle because you do not believe you will get anything or anyone better. You compromise because you do not believe you are worth it or you accept less than what you actually want, because you believe you will never get what you want, anyway.

Sometimes you look at what the man can do or is doing for you and/or your children, i.e. paying the rent, utilities, etc. But although you are unhappy, you settle. You may even, put that man before your children, when you know in truth that you do not want to be with him. You trade your happiness for perceived security or material possessions. You deceive yourself into believing the relationship is for your well-being, yet you have no peace of mind and are miserable. And these are the relationships that many times are loveless.

You settle when you allow the pressure of finding "the one", being married by a certain age, or having children by a certain age, to cause you to compromise and accept a loveless relationship; a relationship that is abusive, where there is no chemistry or attraction, where you are unhappy, or miserable.

You settle if the love you receive does not fulfill your needs. That is, although you may love him deeply, and he may love you, if it is not the love you <u>need</u> then you are settling.

You settle when you love a man who is not there for you emotionally; he is not a shoulder you can lean on, he is emotionally detached. You, therefore, feel as if you are in the relationship by yourself. Do not settle for a man who is emotionally unattached! **By learning to love yourself, you will <u>avoid</u> settling.**

A lack of love for oneself causes you to remain in bondage. Bondage is to be enslaved, to be shackled to someone or something from which you cannot break free. Sometimes you allow verbal, mental, or even physical abuse, because you believe that he loves you. You may even feel that you deserve the abuse. AN ABUSIVE RELATIONSHIP IS A FORM OF BONDAGE. Sometimes you are so desperate to be loved that you accept less than you deserve. Chapter 11 talks about what love is. How love is unconditional. **Love is not abusive.**

A lack of love can create a bitter cycle in your life. A lack of love for oneself creates low self-esteem; low self-esteem causes you to settle and accept a loveless relationship. A loveless relationship is a form of compromise. With compromise, you begin to believe you do not deserve better, which becomes a self-fulfilling prophecy, because you begin to act like you do not deserve better. Believing you do not deserve better perpetuates low self-esteem. Low self-esteem is manifested with a lack of love for oneself. Low self-esteem can cause destructive behavior. Destructive behavior is manifest with a lack of love for oneself; and the cycle continues.

Searching for love in all the <u>wrong</u> places. When there is an absence of love, a void in your life, you begin to search for love. This search is sometimes at a cost and often produces inauthentic love. In addition to accepting relationships that are not for you, that are unhealthy for you, you enter sexual relationships, looking for a man to <u>love</u> you, looking to <u>feel</u> loved. SEX IS <u>NOT</u> LOVE. Many times, these men are using you for sex, because after the sex, they move on and you do not feel valued.

Sometimes you become pregnant, either hoping that the child will create a bond between you and your lover, or you believe the baby will fulfill the lack of love in your life. However, it is more likely that any bond created will only be temporary, that the father will not be in your life, and you will be a single parent. Ultimately, you realize the love you have for your baby does not compare, and is not the same as the love you receive from a man. Unfortunately, you experience hurt and pain when you realize that none of you choices fills the void, and none result in true love.

"You can do bad all by yourself." You do not need a man to do badly, so why remain in a bad relationship? Why stay in an abusive relationship, or with a person that causes you to be unhappy?

Sometimes you allow your pride to keep you in a bad relationship. You are unwilling to hear "I told you so." You are determined to prove to everyone, including yourself, that you did not make a mistake or a bad decision, when in fact, you did.

A lack of love creates an emotional void leading to self-destructive behavior.

- <u>You use sex to fill the void</u>. You become more promiscuous, you engage in indiscriminate sex. You may develop a false sense of pride where you believe "at least I'm good at this <u>one</u> thing." Your sexual prowess goes to your head. You develop an air about your ability to perform well when having sex. Sex becomes a mechanism for control.

Like some men, there are women who prefer being in "sexships", that is relationships that are purely sexual. These woman are not looking for a husband, they want no strings attached; they are just seeking good sex.

- <u>You may use drugs or alcohol to fill the void</u>, to ease the pain, to fulfill the need for love in your life. Then the drug use allows for destructive behavior.

- <u>You over-eat to fill the void</u>. You not only eat because you are hungry, but to comfort yourself. Yet as the weight increases, your sense of self-worth decreases.

These destructive behaviors manifest themselves because of low self-esteem (disbelief that you deserve better), lust, a lack of love in your life, and ultimately, your inability to love yourself. Unfortunately, depression and hence suicidal thoughts are not to be excluded. Lack of love can lead you to a place where you begin to believe your life is not worth it. **YOU ARE <u>WORTH</u> IT!**

Be honest with yourself. Be honest with yourself about your present situation. Are you in a loveless relationship? Do you really want to be in a relationship where you are unhappy? If you do not like your answers, prepare yourself to move on.

Loving yourself does not mean that you are selfish, egotistical or spoiled. Selfishness means you are concerned chiefly with yourself without regards of the well-being of others. You care only about you, exclusive of the feelings, or treatment of others. (You step all over them.) Whereas, loving yourself is being comfortable and accepting of whom you are. **You are not perfect, and it is okay.**

Self-preservation does not mean selfishness. Do not confuse protecting yourself with being selfish. It is wise to be concerned about your safety, and your mental well-being.

You are not a doormat. Do not allow others to walk all over you, take advantage of you, take advantage of your kindness, use you, do what they want with you or to you with blatant disregard for your feelings. Do not let someone just come in and in essence, wipe his feet all over you. You are not a doormat. You deserve to be esteemed, respected, and loved.

Learning to love yourself enables you to receive love from others. When you can accept yourself for who you are, love yourself for who you are, see yourself for the beautiful woman you are, then you will be able to receive love from others, to accept love from others. You will be able to allow someone to love you.

Forgive. You must forgive others. Stop holding on to how you were mistreated in the past. Do not be angry and embittered by what was. Let it go.

> Forbearing one another, and forgiving one another, if any man have a quarrel against any: even as Christ forgave you, so also do ye. (Colossians 3:13, KJV)

Seek forgiveness from God. I John 1:9 – "If we confess our sins, he is faithful and just to forgive us our sins, and to cleanse us from all unrighteousness." When God forgives you, He frees you from the guilt and shame of your past behavior. You are a new creature in Christ. "If any man be in Christ, he is a new creature: old things are passed away; behold, all things are become new." (II Corinthians 5:17, KJV)

When God forgives you, those things you did in the past are forgotten. "I, even I, am the one who wipes out your transgressions for My own sake; and I will not remember your sins." (Isaiah 43:25, KJV) When God forgives you, he throws your sins, the things of your past, into the depths of the sea.

> Who is a God like you, who pardons sin and forgives the transgression of the remnant of his inheritance? You do not stay angry forever but delight to show mercy.
>
> You will again have compassion on us; you will tread our sins underfoot and hurl all our iniquities into the depths of the sea.
> (Micah 7:18-19, NIV)

Forgive yourself. Stop berating yourself. Stop beating up yourself over past mistakes. You cannot change what has occurred yesterday, but you can make better decisions today and tomorrow. Forgiveness will allow you to love others, but more significantly, you will be able to love yourself. "Therefore, I tell you, her many sins have been forgiven—for she loved much. But he who has been forgiven little loves little." (Luke 7:47, NIV)

Only Christ can fill the void. Your children will not fill the void; your job will not fill the void; your mate cannot fill the void. When you accept Jesus Christ as your personal Savior, He meets your deepest love needs. **How do you accept Jesus as your Lord and Savior?**

> That if thou shalt confess with thy mouth the Lord Jesus, and shalt believe in thine heart that God hath raised him from the dead, thou shalt be saved.
>
> For with the heart man believeth unto righteousness; and with the mouth confession is made unto salvation.
>
> For the scripture saith, Whosoever believeth on him shall not be ashamed.

(Romans 10:9-11, KJV)

> For whosoever shall call upon the name of the Lord shall be saved.
> (Romans 10:13, KJV)

When you accept Jesus Christ as your Savior, you belong to God.

> And ye are Christ's; and Christ is God's.
> (I Corinthians 3:23, KJV)

When you accept Jesus Christ as your Savior, you are freed from bondage. When Jesus died on the cross for our sins, we were instantly liberated from the bondage of sin, the bondage of low self-esteem, homosexuality, promiscuity, depression, bitterness, or unforgiveness. Christ is your deliverer. Christ has the power to deliver you from bondage; Christ has the power to set you free. Through Christ, you are free from your past.

> If the Son therefore shall make you free, ye shall be free indeed.
> (John 8:36, KJV)

> Stand fast therefore in the liberty wherewith Christ hath made us free, and be not entangled again with the yoke of bondage.
> (Galatians 5:1, KJV)

It was not until I was introduced to Jesus Christ as my Lord and Savior, that I learned what love is.

> But God commendeth his love toward us, in that, while we were yet sinners, Christ died for us.
> (Romans 5:8, KJV)

I learned how to love, how to be loved, and how to love others.

> Beloved, let us love one another: for love is of God; and every one that loveth is born of God, and knoweth God.
>
> He that loveth not knoweth not God; for God is love.

> In this was manifested the love of God toward us, because that God sent his only begotten Son into the world, that we might live through him.
>
> Herein is love, not that we loved God, but that he loved us, and sent his Son to be the propitiation for our sins.
>
> Beloved, if God so loved us, we ought also to love one another.
> (I John 4:7-11, KJV)

I also learned that nothing can separate us form the love of God, which is through Christ Jesus.

> Who shall separate us from the love of Christ? shall tribulation, or distress, or persecution, or famine, or nakedness, or peril, or sword?
> (Romans 8:35, KJV)

Nay, in all these things we are more than conquerors through him that loved us.

For I am persuaded, that neither death, nor life, nor angels, nor principalities, nor powers, nor things present, nor things to come,

Nor height, nor depth, nor any other creature, shall be able to separate us from the love of God, which is in Christ Jesus our Lord.
(Romans 8:37-39, KJV)

You are Worthy of Love!

Chapter 11: Lust Does Not (≠) Equal Love

Lust and love are two very different emotions, although many people confuse one for the other.

What Lust Is

Lust can be defined as *"Intense or unrestrained sexual craving; sexual desire."*[5] Let us examine this definition.

- Intense – existing in an extreme degree; marked by or expressive of great zeal, energy determination or concentration.[6]

- Unrestrained – immoderate; uncontrolled.[7]

- Craving – an intense, urgent, or abnormal desire or longing.[8]

Lust, pure and simple, is sexual desire. It is that intense sexual attraction, usually without associated feelings of love or affection. When you are lusting after someone, you desire sex with that person, you long for it, you ache for it, you crave it. When you are lusting after some thing, you have a very strong desire to possess that thing. **Lust causes you to behave in ways you often later regret.**

Lust will cause you to have tunnel vision. You goal becomes to sleep with that individual, no matter what, and sometimes regardless of the cost. You set your sights on him, you know you want to sex him and you make it your business to succeed in your pursuit. The lust causes you to seek immediate gratification. The sex is usually hot and heavy, and offers intense satisfaction, BUT you can easily bypass certain safeguards, like using condoms, practicing safe sex, or you even lack regard for your physical safety.

Lust may cause you to be a "freak." It affects what you wear — you dress provocatively; it shapes what you will allow, what you do, and what boundaries you transgress. It is <u>that</u> <u>thing</u> that leads to promiscuous behavior, indiscriminate sex, or illicit sex. It is that thing that induces you to lack restraint, to act in ways that are not subject to your control, and to act uninhibited or without restriction.

Flirting is a form of lust. Flirting is behaving in a playfully alluring way. It may seem innocent enough, but flirting is a manifestation of lust. You use flirtatious behavior to draw attention to yourself. Whether you use it to create sexual appeal, as an indication of attraction, or as a means of manipulation to get what you want, it is still lust that prompts you to flirt. Lust for a person, or lust for the thing you are trying to obtain.

Lust may cause you to have no boundaries, moral or social. You act immoderately, that is you go beyond what is healthy, moral, appropriate, or socially acceptable. Lust causes you to act in a way that is degrading or demeaning to yourself, or to accept behavior that will degrade or demean you. You <u>will</u> attract men, but these men will only want to sleep with you, because they see the lust and will take advantage of it, and you.

Lust causes you to sin against God. "But every man is tempted, when he is drawn away of his own lust, and enticed. Then when lust hath conceived, it bringeth forth sin: and sin, when it is finished, bringeth forth death." (James 1:14, 15, KJV)

What Love Is

"Love is patient, love is kind. It does not envy, it does not boast, it is not proud. It is not rude, it is not self-seeking, it is not easily angered, it keeps no record of wrongs. Love does not delight in evil, but rejoices with the truth. It always protects, always trust, always hopes, always perseveres. Love never fails." (I Corinthians 13:4-8, NIV)

Love is protective; it causes you to feel secure, to feel safe. Love will be giving and caring; it is not selfish; it will not hold things over your head. It causes you to feel esteemed, to feel treasured. Love will be honest, love will be unconditional, and it is longsuffering. Love is authentic and genuine; it will not deceive you. Love will put up with your issues; it will not give up so easily. Love is supportive; Love will always want what is best for you.

Love is an action word. Love is not always what is said; love is not exclusively based on how you feel, but what is manifested, what is demonstrated. It is true that your emotions are involved, but they cannot be your only criteria for love. True love will always lead to actions. "Dear children, let us not love with words or tongue but with actions and in truth." (I John 3:18, NIV) You know what love is by his actions, by how he treats you, by how you treat him. He will <u>show</u> you love. Yes, you want to hear "I love you", but saying it one million times will not make it love.

Love is sharing yourself with another. It is the act of giving your heart. You are committed to that person, your mate, heart, soul, mind and body. When you love someone, then you should desire to please him; you should <u>want</u> to do the things that please him, the things that make him happy. You should desire to support him and to make sure things go smoothly for him. You desire to act selflessly and to give of yourself, to go above and beyond, to give 110% because you care for him, because you love him. It is not just altruism, it is pure unselfish love.

Love is from the heart. It causes you to believe there are no boundaries, that you can conquer anything. You feel you can say anything, do anything, be anything. The thought of him makes your heart feel as if it will burst, that it can jump right out of your chest. The sight or scent of him makes your stomach jump or flutter. When you are not together, your heart aches for him, your heart longs for him. It is more than a feeling, it is a knowing. And NO ONE can tell you <u>who</u> to love!

Love is Respect. Love is consideration, valuing your mate. Valuing his opinions, his dreams, his goals.

Love is not abusive. It will not verbally, mentally, emotionally, or physically abuse or scar you. It will not tear you down, beat you down, disrespect you, berate you, or make you feel less than whom you are, even when you <u>are</u> wrong.

True love is unadulterated. It is pure. It is absolute. It is unconditional. It is a love that never fades, a love that is always with you. It is an abiding love.

True love exists. There are those who will tell you that they have found true love, that they have found the love of their life, their soul mate, their one true love. This is the person who is their morning and evening, their breath in and their breath out, a person with whom they have a connection, with whom they fit, or just click. This is the person that they know they are meant to be with for the rest of their life.

True love is as time goes by, when you look into his eyes, you still see him as what he thinks he still looks like. True love induces you to love a person, even when they are not feeling their best; even when you feel they are not at their best, you still love that person. You can only identify true love and know when you have found it, based on the Word of God. When you match up your relationship to what the Bible says love is, and you are honestly prepared to make a life-long commitment to that person, then you can say that you are truly "in love."

When you encounter this kind of love, when you encounter true love, you are willing to sacrifice all, endure all, surrender all. Neither time, nor distance, not even death, will not diminish your love for him. When true love exists, you know that no matter the circumstances, no matter the outcome, there will always be a place for him in your heart.

True love serves as a barometer for all other love in your life. Once you experience true love, you desire to have it in all of your relationships, and when it is missing, you know it.

True love is the kind of love that God has for us. "For God so loved the world, that he gave his only begotten Son, that whosoever believeth in him shall not perish, but have everlasting life. For God sent not his Son into the world to condemn the world; but that the world through him might be saved." (John 3:16, 17, KJV) Christ was devoted to us enough to give his own life for us. "But God demonstrates his own love for us in this: While we were still sinners, Christ died for us." (Romans 5:8, NIV)

Additionally, the qualities that God looks at are different from those we look at. Where as we look at the outward man – physical appearance, popularity, or wealth, these things do not cause God to love you. "For the Lord seeth not as man seeth; for man looketh on the outward appearance, but the Lord looketh on the heart." (I Samuel 16:7, KJV)

Once you have experienced true love, you understand what love is. Aahh, to be loved with the love of God, changes your life.

Chapter 12: What Men Say

In previous chapters, I have mainly discussed many dos and don'ts regarding topics concerning a woman's behavior as it relates to men. However, I wanted to include a brief chapter sharing some of the men's thoughts. The topics are conversations in which the men explicitly expressed regarding a woman's behavior, the attributes they sought and want in a woman, and things many personally found unattractive.

As you can imagine, there was a gamut of likes and dislikes. Some men found certain traits desirable, while others found those same behaviors completely unappealing. Therefore, I am only including themes for which there was a consensus, because not all men are the same, and beauty <u>really</u> is in the eye of the beholder!

Beyond the outward appearance, and other physical attributes that attract a man to a woman, generally, there are certain characteristics that men say they look for – personality, sense of humor, inward beauty, a kind-hearted and loving woman, friendship, and chemistry. Additionally, there are specific traits that men say they seek.

A man wants a woman who shares his interests. For example, if the man enjoys humor, he wants a woman who likes to laugh. If the man is athletic, he is not necessarily looking for a woman who is a couch potato; he wants a woman who can keep up with him. If he is a sports fanatic, or enjoys watching sports, he would like a woman to have <u>some</u> knowledge of the game, and more significantly, he wants her to allow him to have his time to watch or play the game. It is not as if you did not know that he loves sports, so give him his space!

A man wants a helpmate, not dead weight. A helper comparable to him, as opposed to a woman whom he believes will hinder him from realizing his dreams, or who will hold him back. A man desires someone who will help him fulfill his goals. That woman is someone who is dependable and reliable. He wants a woman who has his back, who will be there for him, who is not selfish or self-centered and who is willing to take up the slack, if needed.

A man wants a woman who is supportive. He is aware that not all of his ideas are perfect.

However, he would appreciate it if his woman would not shoot down every idea he has. It causes him to feel that she is not in his corner, or that she believes he is not good enough for her. It also causes him to believe that he is with a woman that he cannot make happy, one he cannot please, no matter what he tries, no matter how hard he tries. A man wants a woman to be encouraging and a man wants to be encouraged.

A man desires a woman who represents the total package. What man would not want a woman with the complete package? A woman who encompasses or embodies what his ideals of a "good" woman are is paramount. A woman who is smart, intelligent, good looking, sexy; a woman who knows how to represent, who takes care of the home and who also has the "f" factor; that "freak factor". Now, every man has his own interpretation of what a freak is. For example, a freak may be a woman who lacks inhibition or a freak may be a woman who is willing to do things out of the norm; different from the normal routine, but ultimately, she knows how to please him. Although he may not broadcast it, a man wants the package deal designated with an "f".

There are some women that the men said they find unattractive, or who completely turn them off. These women exhibit behaviors that are unappealing, especially when these behaviors manifest at a first meeting, or too early in the relationship. The following are women that the men stated they eventually break off the relationship, completely cut them off, or even <u>avoid</u> entering into a relationship.

- A woman who <u>expects</u> the man to pay her bills.

- A woman who asks if she can move in with him, or "move into his room."

- A woman who asks to be added to his credit card or that he pays her bills with his credit card.

- A woman who is <u>too</u> extreme. She is either <u>too</u> shy, or <u>too</u> aggressive.

- A woman who has incredibly low self-esteem.

- Women who live outside of their means. The men describe this as a woman who moves every 3 months, because she cannot afford her rent.

- A woman who does not know what she wants. The men stated that she acts like she knows what she wants; however, when you give it to her, it's not what she wants, or she doesn't <u>know</u>.

- A woman who tailor-makes herself to get the man she wants. This is the woman that never shows her true colors, who she really is. So the man does not get to know (the real) her.

- A woman who rides a broom. She looks good, she appears to have it all together on the outside. She appears to be classy, she has sensuality, she looks well put together, and people are drawn to her. When she walks into a room all heads turn, everyone stops to look at her. Even when she is not trying, it is just there. She is refined, is educated, speaks correctly, but the moment she opens her mouth the refinement is out the window; all of the sexy drains out of her mouth. The minute she opens her mouth to talk, he realizes she is not the woman for him.

She has an abrasive personality. She is assertive to the point of being abrupt, obnoxious, uncouth and cold. She colors herself ugly. Even though he may look passed the spoken word, passed the initial conversation, and decide he wants to get to know her, the more she talks, the more ugly she appears, which is a complete turn-off. She is classified as a "female dog" by those she turns off.

- A woman who argues with him, or picks fights, just for the make-up sex. It is not as if he does not enjoy the sex, but he can do without the constant bickering.

- A woman who withholds sex, just because she can. She constantly has a headache, or is just not in the mood. She then justifies her behavior by saying he is on punishment for some "perceived" indiscretion.

- A woman who argues, or picks fights to get out of the house. She says she is with her girlfriend(s), but her explanation is a cover to go out with or to meet another man.

- A woman who plays games – mind games, games to test or prove him. The men said they not only find the games to be annoying, unnecessary, and childish, but demonstrative of a lack of maturity, and indicative of a lack of respect for him.

- A woman who is deceptive, dishonest, deceitful, sneaky. A man wants a woman who has character, and integrity, whom he can trust, and he <u>will</u> test you.

- A woman who constantly accuses him of cheating when he is not. She is mistrusting, she snoops, goes through his belongings. She is a woman that creates drama. He cuts her off before she becomes a psycho or a fatal attraction.

- A woman who flips out because he has female friends. Before she was his girlfriend, he had female friends, relationships with women that were platonic (non-sexual); similarly, she has friends who are men. Just because she is now in his life, she should not expect him to drop every friend who is a woman. The truth of the matter is that as the relationship progresses, he will make it known that she is number one. If he respects her, he will not make her feel that those other women come before her.

- A woman who reads more into the relationship than there really is. Yes, he may be attracted to a woman; he may even have feelings for her, but if he has not <u>told</u> her, then SHE IS NOT HIS GIRLFRIEND. She is just a friend. It does not matter that they talk frequently, hang out regularly, flirt, or have sex. If he has not "stated" his intentions, or defined his relationship, then it is likely he is not interested in pursuing a committed relationship with her.

The men agreed that they would introduce the woman based on how they see the relationship – "meet my girlfriend, or fiancé, so and so." As opposed to, "This is Barbara." Who?!? No definition means no commitment.

- A woman who lets her girlfriend(s) dictate her relationship. This was a hot-topic. The men <u>resented</u> having others in their business, to the point that they felt that they were dating the girlfriend. They stated they often grew to *loath* the advice-giver, and could not be friendly with her, and that her interference often caused great strain to the relationship.

- A woman who is not clean. She may look good, she may dress well, and she may appear to be clean, but if she keeps a dirty apartment, or if her home is dirty, then <u>she</u> is considered dirty.

- A woman who is ugly on the inside. No matter the outward appearance, if she is bitter, acerbic, mean-spirited, extremely jealous or envious, then it makes her unattractive.

Conclusion

Relationships require the use of common sense and the application of wisdom, whether you are dating, just friends, in a long-term commitment, or married. Some moments necessitate restraint, while others dictate action, but all-in-all relationships require you to evaluate the situations, and most significantly, evaluate yourself; how you are acting, how you are treating your mate, how he is treating you.

Remain true to yourself and trust your gut. Know when to stay, and do not be afraid to walk away. Let a date be a date. Do not have sex on the first, or second date. In fact, know that you should not have sex before you are married. Learn to listen and hear those around you. Be aware that lust and love are not equal, that relationships come and go, and know that you will overcome your broken heart. Learn to love yourself.

I cannot say that there was a single defining moment that compelled me to write this book. If I were to view my life as an observer, instead of as a participant, I would be able to testify that there were many moments that went into this journey.

Like a panoramic view, there are so many components that affected who I was, and who I have become today. Because life is a constant journey, I am positive there will be additional events that will alter my present existence, which will cause me to grow and to change, prayerfully for the better.

It would be foolish of me to think that you will agree with everything that I have written, but as a wise person once said to me, "In life you eat the meat and discard the bones." That means, you take what applies in your life, use it, pass it on, and discard what does not apply.

Finally, there is only one thing in my life that I have found to be true, and that is the Living Word; the Son of God; Jesus the Christ. Through all of my ups and downs, adventures, misfortunes, and bumps in the road, the Lord has consistently provided what I needed: Himself. And that is LIFE!

> The thief cometh not, but for to steal, and to kill, and to destroy: I am come that they might have life, and that they might have it more abundantly.
> (John 10:10, KJV)

Conclusion

Therefore, if you take nothing else from this book, or from my experiences, my prayer and my hope is that you take, you accept, and receive Jesus Christ as Lord and Savior in your life (see chapter 10) and that he will rule in your relationships, in your decisions, in your choices, and in every area of your life. Again, I encourage in <u>every</u> relationship you have: dating, friendships, long-term commitments, or in marriage, to accept Jesus as your savior, embracing Him and the life He has for you.

He Loves You, Not

Acknowledgements

I first give thanks to my Lord and Savior, Jesus Christ. You are my King and I love you with all my heart, mind, soul, and might. Thank you for another chance, Your mercy, Your love, Your faithfulness and longsuffering.

To the Man of God: thank you for showing me the love of God, for causing me to love and showing me what it means to be a true child of God; thank you for living the truth.

To my friends and family: thank you for your love and support. To my two children, Pastor E.H. Westfield, Pastor Terrence Griffith, Pastor Rich Martin, Vincent Palmer, Betty Norwood, P. Davis, Mr. Bruce, Stacey Cruise, J. Francis, Kris Gaines, Pamela Mitchell, David Gaines, Henry Nesmith, Bill Martin, Byron Sims, William Martin, Leroy Bibbs, Andrea, Mirabelle Griffith (of Barbados, West Indies), to Donielle C. Jones (my talented editor), and A. Jacques: thank you for your encouragement, your advice, your amendments, your editing, but most importantly, for just listening to me reread and re-write paragraphs until I got them right.

- J.B. Tremont

NOTES

[1] Merriam-Webster's Collegiate Dictionary 11th Ed. Merriam-Webster, Inc. USA, 2005

[2] Caselotti, Adriana. "Someday My Prince Will Come." <u>Snow White and the Seven Dwarfs</u>. Disney, 1937

[3] Stevenson RL: Dr. Jekyll and Mr. Hyde (1886). New York, Bantam Books, 1981

[4] Merriam-Webster's Collegiate Dictionary 11th Ed. Merriam-Webster, Inc. USA, 2005

[5] 2nd College Edition, The American Heritage Dictionary, Houghton Mifflin Co., Boston, MA, 1982

[6] Merriam-Webster's Collegiate Dictionary 11th Ed. Merriam-Webster, Inc. USA, 2005

[7] Ibid.

[8] Ibid.

He Loves You, Not

Index of A to Z Topics

abandonment, 118
abuse, 46, 127, 144
acceptance, 34, 35, 62, 70, 117
accepting Jesus Christ, 134
adulterer, 48, 82
adultery, 115
advice, 69, 74
agreement, 25, 29
AIDS, 18, 79
alcohol, 16, 130
anger, 28, 79, 93, 94, 98, 119, 120, 142
appreciation, 35
arguments, 31
attitude, 28
avoidance, 12, 63

baggage, 39, 41, 84, 120
betrayal, 41, 115
bitterness, 119, 127
bondage, 127
   freedom from, 135
booty-call, 13
boundaries, 15, 24, 140, 141
breaking up, 97
break-up sex, 121

change, 35, 36, 92, 109
   adapt to, 34
   dramatic, 36
   fearing change, 91
   personality change, 107

character of men, 46–61
children, 94
Christ's love, 108, 134
commitment, 23, 43, 101
common sense, viii, 11, 62
communication, 23, 25
compromise, 25
conceit, 47
counseling, 123
courage, 43
courtship, 5
coveting, 41

dating, 1, 100
   blind date, 8
   group dating, 9
   solo dating, 7
dating, terms for
   boo lovin, 3
   seeing someone, 3
   talking, 2
deceit, 48
deflection, 49
denial, 63, 69, 112
depression, 117, 130
disappointment, 78, 110, 115
dishonesty, 153
disrespect, 38
distractions, 41
distrust, 14
divorce, 88, 104
dog, 60, 110
drugs, 130

Index

embarrassment, 37
emotional attachment, 91
emotions, 27, 96

failure, 121
faith, 43
fear, 89, 112
fighting, 26
finances, 25
flirting, 141
fool, 71, 110
forcing relationships, 106, 110
forgetting, 118
forgiveness, 33, 119, 132, 133
fornication, 82, 83
freedom, 135
friendship, 101

Godly counsel, 70
God's love, 136, 137, 146
grief, 97, 115, 117, 125
growth, 34
guilt, 49, 80
    freedom from, 81, 132
gut instincts, 45, 61, 62, 112

hardness of heart, 123
hate, 94
healing, 116, 117
helpmate, 148
hindsight, 72
HIV, 18
homosexuality, 79, 135
honesty, 10, 24, 130
hooking-up, 13
humility, 26
hurt, 115

ignorance, 63
integrity, 24, 96

jealousy, 87, 93

lewdness, 51, 79
life, 33
listening, 11, 31, 32, 68
    failure to, 32, 67, 74
long-term goals, 25
love, 136, 142, 144
    lack of, 125, 127, 129
love is blind, 67
loyalty, 101
    lack of, 60
lust, 80, 139, 140, 141
lying, 55, 106

manipulation, 94
marital sex, 81
marriage, 37, 103
micromanagement, 30
mistakes, 65

nagging, 30
negativity, 24, 70

offense, 29
one-night stand, 13, 79
over-eating, 130

past relationships, 28, 39, 40
perseverance, 42
personal information, 10, 16
pettiness, 94
possessiveness, 87, 92
power tripping, 31
premarital sex, 78
pride, 26, 129
problems, 63, 72, 79, 91, 94, 106
promiscuity, 14, 77, 79, 129

reality, 6, 33
rebound relationships, 122

Index

regret, 13, 20, 80, 96, 121, 140
   freedom from, 81
rejection, 11, 12, 33, 46, 115, 122
relationship flow chart, 105
repercussions, 98
respect, 15, 21, 24
romance, 36

searching for love, 128
self-absorption, 47
self-control, 20
self-destructive behavior, 129
self-esteem, 90, 95, 120, 125, 127, 130, 131, 135, 150
self-evaluation, 34
selfishness, 131
selflessness, 35
self-love, 125, 131, 132
self-preservation, 131
self-restraint, 121
self-worth, 22, 109
settling, 112, 122, 125
sex, 13, 15, 92, 129
sexships, 77, 130
sexual activity, 77, 78
sexual desire, 139

sin, 141
soul mate, 144
stalking, 46
standards, 19
STDs, 18, 79
strength, 43
stress, 57
stupidity, 74
submission, 27
support, 148

tradition, 88
true love, 144, 145
trust, 41
   lack of, 40
truth, 61, 69, 117
turn-offs, 150–56

understanding, 23, 24, 34
unfaithfulness, 90
unhappiness, 93, 112, 126, 129, 131
unprotected sex, 18

value, 21
vulnerability, 28

waiting, 19, 20, 84
warning, 39, 62, 63, 67, 73

www.ingramcontent.com/pod-product-compliance
Lightning Source LLC
Chambersburg PA
CBHW060533100426
42743CB00009B/1517